How To Make 17/18 Profit Days In 22 Trading Days

Simple and easy hacks to become pro - trader

PANKAJ SAHU

BlueRose ONE.com
Stories Matter
NewDelhi • London

BLUEROSE PUBLISHERS
India | U.K.

BlueRose ONE
Stories Matter
New Delhi • London

For permissions requests or inquiries regarding this publication, please contact:

BLUEROSE PUBLISHERS
www.BlueRoseONE.com
info@bluerosepublishers.com
+91 8882 898 898
+4407342408967

ISBN: 978-93-7310-990-9

Cover design: Aman Sharma
Typesetting: Manisha Rawat

First Edition: November 2025

"If you decide your stop loss then profit is unlimited in stockmarket"

Pankaj sahu

Contents

My Journey: From Novice to Consistent Trader

About Me

This line, "About Me," the answer to it lies with you. Ten years ago, I was exactly where you are now. Yes, you might think this is a very short answer, but that's it. Because I won't narrate my entire journey from childhood to where I am now in my youth. I'll start from where my struggle began, where I became aware, and where I started doing everything, started working hard. That's where I'll begin telling you.

If I start talking about myself, I'd have to publish another book. Because my life has seen many ups and downs. I've witnessed many tragic moments and many happy ones too. It's like a movie, you know? Every person's life is like a movie, and mine was no different. Ups and downs, and it's still ongoing. But let me tell you about my beginnings. When I became aware, when I started struggling.

In 2011, I completed my MBA from IMS Ranchi, Institute of Management Studies. I've always been an average student. I never really had a keen interest in studies. I was always a backbencher, or even further back if there was a bench behind the backbenchers, that's where I'd sit. I did my MBA because at home, it was expected to become an engineer or do an MBA, like everyone else. So, when my father suggested I do an MBA, I did it. My percentile was around fifty-five or sixty, which is why no company would hire me. You know how it is if your percentage is that low. I didn't get a job in Ranchi, so I went to Delhi to look for one. Because after doing an MBA, there's a burden to get a job. So, I had to get a job, and I went to Delhi.

In 2011, I searched and searched, but who would hire someone with such low percentages? I was still taking money from home. There came a time when I felt ashamed of taking money from home after four or five months without a job. So, I lied to my family, saying I got a job, but I hadn't. Eventually, I did get a job at a multinational company, earning twelve thousand rupees, where I had to sell Tata Sky and Videocon set-top boxes door-to-door. I earned commissions from that, and my target was to sell five times the twelve thousand rupees to get paid. I managed to sell twelve or thirteen thousand in the first couple of months, and the company, out of pity, paid me for a couple of months.

During that time, I developed an interest in the stock market because I met a couple of colleagues who invested and traded in the stock market. I used to hear about it, that there was something called the stock market. So, I worked for three or four months. Sometimes I met my targets, sometimes I didn't. There was a time when I survived in Delhi for seven days on just "mathri" (a type of biscuit) and tea because I had no money left after paying rent and other expenses. I had stopped asking for money from home.

My family has always been very supportive and capable, and having a supportive family is very important. My father always supported me, whether financially or otherwise. Then I developed a bit of interest because, you know, who doesn't want quick money? Some of my colleagues were investing and trading in the stock market, so I thought I'd give it a try too. I had no initial learning, so I started swing trading. I had saved fifty to sixty thousand rupees over five or six months from commissions, and I started swing trading with that. I did swing trading for two or three months. With a small capital, you can't make big profits, and I didn't understand that. I was just paying brokerage fees and getting frustrated that I wasn't making money.

Then I heard about options trading. I heard about Nifty options trading, where a premium of 10 or 20 rupees could suddenly become 200 or 300 rupees, and your five or ten thousand capital could turn into a lakh. There was no YouTube back then, no books either, so I had no idea. I opened an account for options trading and started trading options. I only knew about call and put options. I started random trading, and believe it or not, within ten days, I turned my forty to fifty thousand capital into seventy-five thousand by gambling and randomly buying calls and puts. I became overconfident.

I started dreaming that now big profits would start coming in, and I'd quit my job. I wouldn't have to work hard anymore. I'd focus on trading and grow my capital. I'd earn one or two lakhs a month, twelve to thirteen lakhs, fifteen lakhs a year. I'd have a BMW, a house. I started dreaming all these dreams. But I had a small capital. So, I told my father that I was going to start a small startup in Delhi and needed three and a half lakhs. He arranged it for me. My father has always been supportive and never said no to anything. He arranged it, and I combined it with my capital and started options trading.

For five or six days, I was scared because it was a huge capital. I'm talking about ten to twelve years ago when books were being printed. But one day, there was an expiry in Nifty. What happens is that the premium becomes zero on that day, and a lot of money can be made. I got a tip that the market was going to open with a big gap the next day, and I was dreaming of becoming a multi-billionaire, making big profits. I remember holding a call option worth three lakh forty thousand for the next day. I got a tip that the market would open with a big gap the next day, and I held the call option. I couldn't sleep that night.

When the market opened the next day, it opened with a gap down, and my loss started at minus fifty thousand, which I had never seen before. I started sweating because I had never imagined such a big loss. That's when my hope trading began, hoping that the market would go up and my loss would be recovered. I prayed to God, promising to offer flowers and other things if my loss was recovered. Those who have experienced losses can understand the emotional pain. I just wanted my loss to be recovered, and I promised not to trade like that again. That day was Nifty's expiry. I kept hoping and trading, but the premium kept melting, and the loss kept increasing. It reached a lakh, and my mind froze. What to do? If I exited, I'd be at a lakh's loss, which I had never seen before. It would take me two or three years to earn a lakh. With hope trading, my loss kept increasing, and the market was stuck. That day, I gave the market three lakh forty thousand, making my entire capital zero. It was the most dramatic situation of my life. Three lakh forty thousand was a big amount for me, and it still is for many people. For a middle-class family, and because I had taken it from my father, the entire capital of three lakh forty thousand became zero.

For five or six days, I didn't eat or drink anything. I didn't talk to anyone. My father would call, but I wouldn't answer. But one thing was, that my father was very supportive. I told him that I had lost all the money by doing this. He immediately said, "Come back home from Delhi. There's no problem; we'll start again." But I had decided that if I had to do something, it would be this, or nothing at all. Most people, when they incur losses, exit the market. I didn't do that. I decided that I would do this, stock market trading, or nothing at all. I started studying from there. I said I would study, learn everything, and then trade. I started reading a lot of books. I read books by famous authors like Frank Ochoa, Mark Douglas, Jesse Livermore, Peter Lynch. I read all the books related to the stock market, psychology, and trading within six months. My basics to advanced knowledge became so clear that I could teach someone else. But my psychology part wasn't developing.

I started searching on YouTube. By then, YouTube had started growing a bit. I found some videos and references, and I discovered the US market. I found a mentor in the US market and connected with them. I started studying a bit about crypto and forex. Since I had already read books, I connected with them, and they told me to join them. They would help develop my psychology and setup. I paid them a hundred dollars for the study and joined them. They explained everything to me so well. There were others with me too. They helped develop my psychology and setup. They taught me many things, like when to trade and when not to trade. In the US market, Indian market, any market, if your psychology is strong, no market is small for you.

You can trade in any market. Psychology is the most important part of your trading journey. I understood this in ten years. Eighty percent of it is psychology, which includes fear, greed, emotions, and revenge. Only twenty percent is the setup, and people chase setups but don't focus on building their psychology. I understood this.

After getting their guidance, my psychology started developing well. I started gaining patience and discipline. Then I started making small profits in the crypto and forex markets. I started building my capital in the Indian market. I followed it for three or four years, growing my capital little by little. I grew it to four or five lakhs in crypto, and I continued regularly. I kept learning and earning. It was enough to run the household, but a big reform wasn't coming in my life. I could take care of my family, but a big reform wasn't happening. The reform in my life came in 2020 because, you see, you can't stay stuck in one thing forever; you have to move forward.

I created my own personal setup, the Lord Loren Setup. What is the Lord Lawrence Setup? I've already mentioned it in this book. After creating this setup, my entire life changed. I worked on it for six months, designed everything, tested it, backtested it, and made it of such high quality. I traded with confidence for three to four years, and my friends and family started trading, building their capital. Now, I'm managing a portfolio of 14 crores in 2025. This setup was so powerful in my life, and then a stage of self-actualization comes when you feel that this setup shouldn't just be with you. It should be with those who want to trade and generate income.

SEBI conducted research that showed 90 percent of people are making losses. With this setup, I realized that you can't make losses. I'm not saying you'll make a profit every day, but I guarantee 200 percent that your portfolio will be green every month if you follow some setups and risk management. This is what I developed with this setup, and then you know the rest of the story. I started my YouTube channel, began mentoring people, and more and more people joined me. Today, I have more than 120,000 YouTube subscribers, and my Lawrence Community has more than 10,000 members. I've taught over 20,000 people so far. I've received a lot of recognition, including from Dhan, and I'm also an NSC and BSE registered, SEBI registered, and an authorized person of MCX, NSE, and BSE. I've received many recognitions and awards for creating the Lawrence Setup, and now I'm mentoring more than 10,000 people who join me live.

For the last two years, I've had the idea of writing this book, and my initiative has always been to make every household a trader. Why are people chasing private jobs and government jobs? There's such a big opportunity in the stock market, and they're missing out. What do you need here? In these ten years, I've learned that you only need two things: a setup that works 80 to 90 percent of the time and a mentor who can develop your psychology. This book mentions all of that.

So, this was a short intro about me, and in this book, you'll see, learn, and understand many more things. This is my ten years of hard work that I'm writing about, so enjoy this book, and by following the things in this book, I don't think anyone's portfolio will be in the red. Every month, their portfolio will be 200 percent green.

Whom is this book for....

Who is this book for? Who should read this book? I think every human being should read this book because it is a universal book. In my opinion, nothing in life is more important than being financially free. So, if you get the knowledge to become financially free from somewhere, you should never miss that opportunity. And this, I have fully defined in this book. I have created this book in such a way that it includes all my learnings and observations about the market from the last ten years, including psychology and setups.

The first few chapters, about seven or eight, will provide you with basic learning. After that, it moves on to an advanced level. So, those who are basic learners can skip the initial chapters and follow the last chapters.

And here is who should read this book. This book is for those who want to generate passive income in life, those who are already frustrated with trading, and those who want to make trading a second source of income. It's for those who want to live a luxurious life and make life happy and enjoyable. This book is for those who have already suffered significant losses in trading. There is no age barrier in this book, and there is no age barrier in trading either. So, anyone who is a human being can read this book because nothing is more important in life than this.

There is a saying that if you have money, you have everything. Many people have their opinions that money isn't everything. But my opinion is that while money isn't everything, without money, there is nothing. So, money is a very important thing, and if you are born as a human, you have the right to earn money, and not just a little, but a lot. Trading skill is such a rare skill that if you develop it, you become a walking ATM. In this book, I have explained everything about how you can become a walking ATM.

I'm not saying that reading this book will work magic. Look, I can show you the roadmap, but you have to apply it. And I guarantee you, I give you a two-hundred percent guarantee. I'm not saying you'll make a profit daily, but after reading this book and following what is explained in it, after following all the setups in this book, I give you a two-hundred percent guarantee that your monthly portfolio will always be in the green. It will never be in the red any month. I give you a two-hundred percent guarantee of this, whether you are a beginner, advanced, or intermediate, no matter what kind of trading you do, no matter what age or stage you are at, no matter what you are doing. This book is for everyone. This is a universal book. So, everyone should read this book. Everyone should read it because after this, you won't need to read any other book related to trading. Just by following what is written in this book, you can achieve everything, and you have the right to achieve it.

I have created this book with a lot of effort. I spent two to three years writing it and shared my ten years of experience. So, read this book with your heart. Yes, those who are a bit of a beginner can start reading this book from the beginning. Yes, those who are a bit advanced can skip the beginner steps because, in the beginning, I have explained the basics like how to take calls and puts, what candlesticks are, what chart patterns are. I have provided all the basic knowledge, like what magnetics are. But in the end, what I have shared is something that everyone, whether a beginner, advanced, or an expert, should read and follow.

Before moving forward in this book, it is very important for you to read this.

Ninety-five percent of people believe that the Indian stock market opens at 9:15 AM and closes at 3:30 PM in the evening. But if I speak honestly, this is a myth. For disciplined traders, for super traders, the market starts even before 9:15 AM. And that's exactly what I'll explain to you—what you need to do before 9:15 AM.

Think of it this way: if you go to war without preparation, without being mentally and physically fit, you're bound to lose. The market is similar. In the market, you analyze, but you also face immense mental pressure. Your heartbeat fluctuates rapidly during trading—how do you control that? People focus on everything else, like making money, but they don't focus on themselves. They spend 24 hours thinking about others. You need to dedicate one hour daily to yourself if you want to survive in the market for the long term.

There are certain practices I'll explain, which I personally apply in my life. I've been following them for the last eight years. If you apply them, you'll become mentally and physically strong. Because, as you know, in the market, 80% of success depends on psychology, and only 20% depends on the setup. If your 80% psychological aspect isn't strong—things like fear, greed, revenge, regret, FOMO—then even if you get a 99.9% perfect setup, you'll still incur losses in the market.

So, the time before 9:15 AM, that one hour, is crucial. How do you divide that one hour? It depends on what time you wake up in the morning. Whether it's 7 to 8 AM or 6 to 7 AM, you need to dedicate one hour to yourself to become mentally and physically strong. This one hour, these 60 minutes, should be divided into three parts: 15 minutes, 15 minutes, and 30 minutes.

In the first 15 minutes, sit quietly and meditate. You can also do breathing exercises because, as you know, if you're not mentally fit, your heartbeat will spike when you take trades—whether you're making a profit or facing a loss. If this continues, you could end up with heart issues, so you need to control it. For the first 15 minutes, practice breathing exercises to calm your mind. You can follow the 6-7-5 rule: inhale for six seconds, hold for seven seconds, and exhale for five seconds. Practice this quietly and consistently for 15 minutes.

For the next 15 minutes, read a book. It can be motivational, devotional, or any book you like, but avoid reading negative news. Always focus on positive news and motivational books. Reading these will help prepare your mind and make it stronger.

The last 30 minutes are the most important. If you're a trader, you spend four to five hours studying and analyzing the market. But this often means your body doesn't get any physical activity. So, in the morning, dedicate 30 minutes to physical activity. You can jog, walk, do yoga, or go to the gym—whatever works for you. Use these 30 minutes to strengthen your body physically.

If you consistently follow this routine, the time after 9:15 AM will become much more productive, and you'll build a strong foundation for yourself. Many people believe the market starts at 9:15 AM and ends at 3:30 PM, but for a trader, the market starts before 9:15 AM and ends by 10 AM. If you want to become a disciplined, profitable, and super trader, never miss this one hour. If you practice this daily, you'll find that everything else becomes easier for you.

Continue this routine and start reading books with this mental state. You'll notice significant changes in your life. These changes will help you achieve profits not just for 17-18 days but potentially even more.

Chapter 1
Fundamentals of Options Trading in India

Introduction: From Stories to Structures

In the last chapter I shared the stumbles, sleepless nights, and small wins that pushed me from a frustrated screen-watcher to a trader who finally saw steady green. You saw the human side—the doubts, the losses, the ah-ha moments when a pattern clicked. Now it is time to put flesh on that narrative skeleton. We shift from the "why" of my journey to the "what" and "how" of the instrument that changed everything for me: options.

Options may look like complicated beasts at first glance, especially in the Indian market where regulatory nuances, taxation, and margin rules all add layers of jargon. Yet once the terminology is demystified, an option is nothing more than a flexible, risk-controlled bet on future price movement. In this chapter, I will hand you the vocabulary, the market structure, the regulatory guardrails, and the first taste of option Greeks. By the time we are done, you will be equipped to open an option chain, recognize a sensible trade, and understand how buying a Bank Nifty CE (Call European style) at 43,000 and hedging with a PE (Put European style) is more than just a random hunch. It's a calculated, rules-based play.

Let's dig in.

---

1. Options 101: What Exactly Is an Option?

An option is a derivative contract—its value "derives" from an underlying asset. In India, the underlying can be an index like Nifty 50 or Bank Nifty, or an individual stock such as Reliance or TCS.

At the center is a simple promise:

• A CALL option gives its buyer the right, but not the obligation, to BUY the underlying at a predetermined price (strike) on or before a predetermined date (expiry). • A PUT option gives its buyer the right, but not the obligation, to SELL the underlying at a predetermined strike on or before expiry.

That "right but not obligation" phrase is critical. If exercising the right makes no economic sense—imagine buying a call on Bank Nifty at 44,000 when the index dumps to 41,500—you simply let the option expire worthless. Your loss is capped at the premium you paid.

Conversely, the writer (seller) of that call or put accepts an obligation. If you sell a 43,000 Bank Nifty call, you must deliver a cash-settlement if the index expires above 43,000, and you will owe the difference. The reward for taking on that obligation is the premium you collect upfront.

---

2. Key Building Blocks of an Option Contract

• UNDERLYING: Index (Nifty 50, Bank Nifty, FIN Nifty, Sensex) or stock.• STRIKE PRICE: The level at which the right kicks in (42,000, 43,500, etc.).• EXPIRY: Weekly for indices and most actively traded stocks, monthly for all, plus quarterly and longer-dated LEAPs in some cases.• LOT SIZE: Number of units per contract (e.g., Bank Nifty = 15 units; Nifty 50 = 50; stock lots vary).• PREMIUM: The price you pay or receive. Moves continually until expiry. • STYLE: Indian index and stock options are European style—exercise happens only on expiry date. • SETTLEMENT: Cash-settled for indices; compulsory physical delivery for stocks in the last week of expiry since October 2019.

A quick anecdote: My first option trade was an 850-strike Call on Infosys back in 2013 when the lot size was 250. I paid ₹9,000 premium and felt dizzy— "Imagine if all 250 shares run 10%!" They didn't. In fact, the stock flat-lined, IV (implied volatility) crashed post-results, and I lost nearly all the premium by Friday. The lesson? Premium is not just about direction; time and volatility matter. Hence the Greeks.

---

3. Where the Action Happens: Exchanges and Ecosystem

NSE vs BSE• National Stock Exchange (NSE) dominates volume in derivatives, >95 % on most days. • Bombay Stock Exchange (BSE) has Sensex and Bankex options but liquidity is thin.

Clearing Corporation• NSE Clearing Ltd (formerly NSCCL) handles margin collection, mark-to-market settlement, and risk management. • Acts as counterparty so you never worry about the buyer/seller defaulting.

Regulator• Securities and Exchange Board of India (SEBI) writes the rules: margin, position limits, physical settlement, and option chain disclosure. • Periodically tweaks lot sizes, introduces new expiries (Bank Nifty moved from Thursdays to Wednesdays in 2023, for instance).

Brokers• Full-service vs discount. The latter (Zerodha, Upstox, Angel One, Fyers) exploded in popularity post-2016. Most of you reading this probably have a discount account; low brokerage keeps your break-even manageable.

Data Vendors• NSE website for live option chain (free).• Paid APIs/terminals (TrueData, GDFL, Sensibull, Opstra) for advanced Greeks, OI analytics, back-testing.

---

4. Why Options Resonate with Indian Traders

Leverage with Defined RiskBuying a call at ₹200 premium on Bank Nifty gives exposure to ~₹6.5 lakh of notional value for ₹3,000 (₹200 × lot size 15). Where else can you control such a position with sub-1 % capital outlay and limited downside?

Volatility PlaygroundBank Nifty's daily swing often exceeds 1.5 %, providing intraday opportunities. Option prices, especially weekly expiries, react violently—ripe for disciplined traders.

Weekly Expiries = Faster Feedback LoopWe used to wait a full month; now we test, refine, and collect data every Wednesday (Bank Nifty) and Thursday (Nifty).

Hedge Against Portfolios. A farmer in Punjab insures his crop; a mutual-fund investor can buy Nifty puts before an RBI policy or global event.

Regulatory Scrutiny Keeps Rogue Players at BayMargin frameworks like SPAN + Exposure, peak margin rules, and physical settlement may feel restrictive but actually protect retail from blowing up instantly.

---

5. Premium Drivers: The Option Pricing Ingredients

Imagine you bake a cake. Flour, sugar, eggs, and heat decide the outcome. For an option, the ingredients are:

• Spot Price of Underlying• Strike Price• Time to Expiry (T)• Volatility (σ)• Risk-Free Interest Rate (r)• Expected Dividends (for stocks)

The Black-Scholes model blends these into a fair value. We don't need to solve differential equations on the trading floor, but you must appreciate that the premium expands with time and volatility, contracts with decay, and flips with the underlying.

A fun analogy: buying a call on a rainy monsoon Tuesday is like grabbing a last-minute movie ticket. If the film is hyped (high IV) and it's opening day (plenty of time value), you pay a hefty premium in the black market. Wait until next week, once reviews cool (IV crush), and that ticket could go for half.

---

6. Meet the Greeks: Your Option's Personality Traits

We traders anthropomorphize options. "This long straddle is theta-bleeding." "My short put is delta-heavy." Below are the personality traits—mathematically derived but practically intuitive.

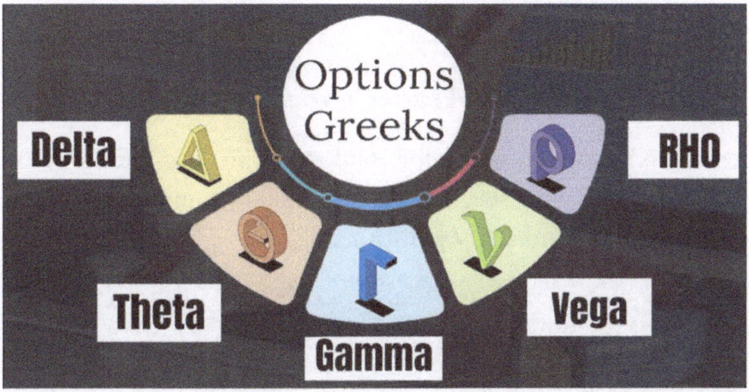

DELTA (Δ): The option's sensitivity to a ₹1 move in the underlying.• Call deltas range 0 to 1; put deltas 0 to -1.• A Bank Nifty 200-point ITM call might have $\Delta \approx 0.6$, meaning if Bank Nifty rallies 100 points, the premium rises roughly ₹60 (ignoring other shifts).

GAMMA (Γ): The delta's sensitivity to underlying moves.• High for ATM (At The Money) weekly options near expiry.• Explains why a small underlying jump suddenly makes your call surge faster: delta itself is growing.

THETA (Θ): Time decay per day.• Negative for buyers, positive for sellers.• On Tuesday night of expiry week, an ATM Bank Nifty option can lose >35 % of its value overnight due solely to theta.

VEGA (ν): Sensitivity to volatility.• Buy options before an event (Budget) when IV is relatively low, anticipate a spike.• If IV collapses after the event, vega works against you even if direction is right.

RHO (ρ): Sensitivity to interest rates.• Minor for short-dated contracts in India, but worth noting for LEAPs.

Quick story: During the 2020 lockdown, the market froze at lower circuits. I bought an April ATM put on Nifty at IV 120. Two hours later the RBI announced aggressive measures; IV fell to 90 even though the index drifted lower. My premium *fell* despite being right on direction. Vega cut me deep. Lesson learned.

---

7. Option Chains: The Trader's Dashboard

Open the NSE option chain for Bank Nifty (or use a terminal with streaming data). You see strikes, premium, volume, open interest, and Greek's (on third-party platforms)

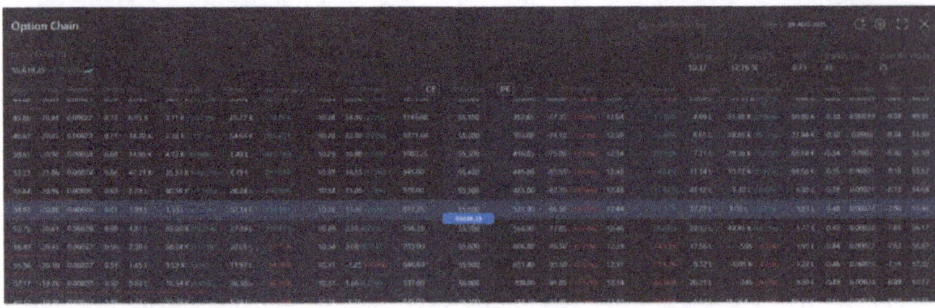

How to read it:

• CALLS on left, PUTS on right.• Yellow shaded = underlying spot ± 3 strikes (ATM region).• Note OI build-up. High OI at 43,000CE and 42,000PE might hint at resistance/support, but keep mindset flexible—big money shifts during the session.

My practice ritual: Every morning at 9:10 a.m. I scan OI changes from the previous session, along with SGX Nifty cues. I annotate two probable magnet strikes for the day. It's like marking goal-posts before the football match begins.

---

8. Buying Calls (CE) and Puts (PE) in Bank Nifty: A Case Study

Let's walk through a trade I placed on 15 March. The strategy: Intraday momentum play via weekly options.

• Set-up: Bank Nifty broke a descending trendline on the 15-minute chart; RSI crossing 60; broader market strong.• Plan: Buy 43,200CE at ≈ ₹220 premium, target ₹340; stop-loss ₹150 (delta ≈ 0.46).• Position Size: 4 lots (15 units each) = 60 units; risk per lot ₹70 → total risk ₹4,200.• Greeks Snapshot: Gamma 0.025, Theta -6/day, Vega 12.

Execution and Management:— 09:45 a.m. Bought 4 lots @ ₹222.— 10:05 a.m. Underlying popped 110 points; premium printed ₹315. Shifted stop to entry to protect capital.— 10:20 a.m. Trailing stop hit @ ₹295. Net profit ≈ ₹4,380 after brokerage and STT.

Observations:

Delta expansion: moved from 0.46 to 0.58 as price neared ITM.

Gamma spiked because less time remained until Wednesday expiry, favoring intraday momentum.

Theta negligible within 45 minutes, validating the "scalp the pop" approach.

You can mirror the same structure on the downside with PEs when the index slices through support or shows bearish divergence.

---

9. Buying vs Selling: Two Sides of the Option Coin

• BUYER

Limited risk (premium), unlimited profit.

Needs significant move before theta erodes value.

Useful for event trades or breakout momentum.

• SELLER (Writer)

Limited profit (premium), potentially large risk.

Benefits from time decay and IV crush.

Must maintain sufficient margin and have disciplined risk management.

Example: Writing a 44,500CE when Bank Nifty is at 42,900 might look safe. But one surprise RBI rate cut and the index can sprint 4 % in two sessions. The seller now either scrambles to buy back at a loss or hedges with futures. We'll dive deeper into spreads and risk containment in Chapter 10, but recognize early that naked selling can be a minefield.

---

10. Margins, Span, and Peak: The Money You Must Park

SEBI rules split margin into SPAN (risk based) and Exposure (additional buffer). Post-2021 you must have full 100 % of margin upfront; no more end-of-day juggling.

Margin Snapshot (approximate):• Selling one lot Bank Nifty ATM call/put: ₹100,000–₹110,000.• Buying same option: premium only, roughly ₹2,000–₹3,000.

Hedged PositionsSell 43,000CE and buy 44,000CE → margin drops to ~₹40,000 because risk is capped.

Takeaway: Margin benefits incentivize spreads over naked shorts, aligning with risk discipline.

---

11. Physical Settlement for Stock Options—Implications

Since October 2019, all stock options result in compulsory delivery in the final week. If you hold an in-the-money Reliance 2600PE on expiry:

• As a buyer: You must deliver 250 shares (lot size) or square off.• As a seller: You must accept 250 shares.

Most retail traders prefer to square off or roll over positions before the delivery window. Index options remain cash-settled—you need not worry about owning 15 units of Bank Nifty (impossible!).

---

16. From Fundamentals to Risk Mastery: What Comes Next

Understanding calls, puts, and Greeks is half the equation. The other half—maybe the more critical—is risk management. I can't overstate how many talented chartists burn out because they ignore position sizing or let a losing trade mutate into a portfolio killer.

In the next chapter, we will dissect risk like surgeons: position sizing formulas, stop-loss placement, and capital protection frameworks that ensure you live to fight another day. Options offer leverage; risk management offers survival. Pair them, and you have the makings of a professional trader.

Grab a coffee, breathe in, and prepare to meet the uncompromising pillar of trading success: risk.

Chapter 2
Understanding Risk: The Pillar of Trading Success

A Quick Look Back—and a Short Step Ahead

In the previous chapter, we explored the nuts and bolts of options trading in India. You now know what an option is, how it is traded on the NSE, and which basic terms you must speak fluently before placing even a single order. But knowing what an option is and making money from trading it are two very different things.

Today I want to take you behind the curtain and talk about the single topic that turned my own account around from "yo-yo" equity curves to steady growth: **risk management**. If you and I master the *when*, *where*, and *how much* of risking capital, the *what* (puts, calls, Bank Nifty, Nifty, stocks) becomes almost secondary.

Why Most Traders Fail (and Why You Won't)

I started out exactly like many retail option traders:

I knew the payoff diagrams.

I could recite every Greek letter from delta to theta.

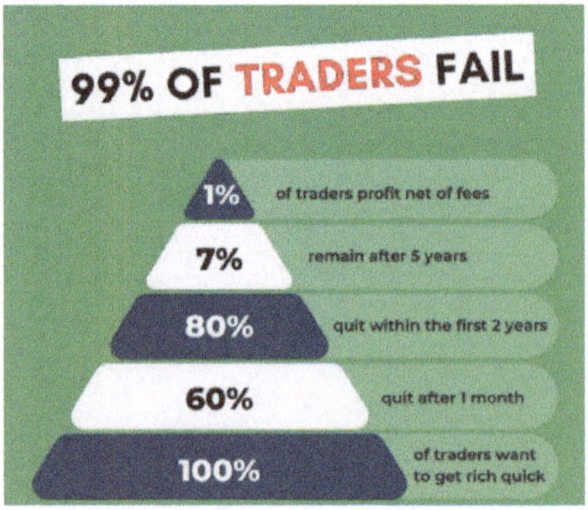

I watched price tick by tick.

And I still lost money. Then one evening my mentor told me: "You don't have a trading problem; you have a **risk** problem." That sentence rewired my entire trading brain. I realised all my chart patterns, market views, and price targets meant nothing if my risk sizing was off by even a small margin.

By the end of this chapter, you will know:

How to decide the *exact* rupee amount you can afford to lose on any trade.

Why a **Daily 1 Trade Rule** can act like a shock absorber for your emotions.

How a **Trailing Stop-Loss (SL)** converts a good entry into a great exit.

What I call the **God Box Theory**—a simple mental exercise that locks in discipline.

A full real-time case study on Bank Nifty options applying everything above.

Let's get started, one careful step at a time.

2.1 The Core Equation: Risk First, Reward Second

Most traders invert the order. They start with, "How much can I make?" You and I will instead ask, "How much can I *lose* and still sleep well?" The paradox is that once you protect the downside, the upside very often looks after itself.

3.1.1 Defining Risk in Plain English

Risk is the amount of money, time, and emotional bandwidth you are willing to stake on a trading idea. It is *not* a vague fear. It is a specific rupee number and a clear exit plan.

Example:You buy a Bank Nifty 45000 Call at ₹200 premium. You decide that if the option drops to ₹150 you will exit. Your risk per lot is therefore ₹50 × 25 (lot size) = ₹ 1,250. Simple, visible, measurable.

3.1.2 The Two Pillars of Personal Risk Tolerance

Financial Capacity – the part of your capital you can lose without changing your lifestyle.

Emotional Capacity – the part of your mind that can accept a loss without revenge-trading.

If either pillar is weak, the house collapses. You must **honour the weaker pillar**. If your wallet can handle a ₹ 5,000 loss but your mind panics beyond ₹ 2,000, your real limit is ₹ 2,000.

3.2 Position Sizing: How Big Is Too Big?

Position sizing is the art of answering, "How many lots should I trade?"

3.2.1 Fixed Rupee Model

Risk a set rupee amount per trade (say ₹ 2,000). To find the number of lots:

Identify entry price and stop-loss price.

Calculate risk per lot.

Divide your ₹2 000 by the risk per lot to get lots.

Example:Entry: ₹180; SL: ₹160; Risk per lot = ₹20 × 25 = ₹500.Lots = ₹2 000 / ₹500 = 4 lots (100 contracts).

3.2.2 Percentage of Capital Model

Risk a small percentage (1 % or 2 %) of total capital per trade.

Capital: ₹5 00 000 Risk per trade @1 %: ₹5 000

Same calculation; only the rupee limit floats as capital grows.

3.2.3 The 30-Trade Cushion

Take your total account size and divide by 30. That figure tells you the maximum *loss per trade* that guarantees you survive at least thirty consecutive losing trades—a near-impossible streak, but the exercise humbles you.

3.3 The Daily 1 Trade Rule: Less Is More

When I was losing money, I took *many* trades, believing frequency equals profitability. My mentor challenged me to a "30-Day One-Trade-A-Day" experiment. My P/L stabilised almost overnight. Here's how you can apply it.

3.3.1 Mechanics of the Rule

Every trading day, you are allowed exactly **one new position**.

You may manage open trades (trail SL, book partial profits), but you cannot open a second fresh trade that day.

If your planned setup fails to appear, you sit out the day—capital intact.

3.3.2 Why It Works

Forces you to wait for *A-grade* setups.

Cuts the temptation of chasing price.

Gives you ample mental space to monitor the open position closely.

Simplifies journaling: one clear decision to review per day.

3.3.3 Adapting for Part-Time Traders

If you have a day job, one trade a day is a blessing. You check the market at a pre-defined time—for instance, 9:25 a.m., after the opening volatility stabilises—place your order with automated SL and target, and then log off.

3.4 Stop-Loss Mastery: Hard, Soft, and Trailing

A stop-loss is an order that closes your position once the price reaches a predetermined level. There are three broad flavours:

Hard SL – fixed price; no discretion.

Soft SL – a zone; you accept some flexibility.

Trailing SL – a stop that moves in your favour as the price advances.

3.4.1 Hard SL

I often start a trade with a hard SL: an absolute "Eject!" button. It lives on the broker's system, away from my temptation to move it.

3.4.2 Switching to a Trailing SL

Once the price moves half the distance to my target, I switch to a trailing SL. This converts paper profits into *protected* profits.

Simple trailing formulas you can use:

Fixed Step Trail – Move SL by ₹10 every ₹10 gain.

Indicator Trail – Use 5-minute 20-EMA as dynamic support/resistance.

Swing Low/High Trail – Place SL below the most recent swing low (for long trades) or above swing high (for shorts).

3.4.3 The Risk-Free Moment

The happiest moment in any trade is when your trailing SL lies at your entry price plus brokerage. You now have zero downside. Psychologically this is liberating; you can hold for the original target or let a trend runner ride.

3.5 The God Box Theory: Containing the Beast

You may wonder, "What on earth is a God Box?" It is simply a *mental container* in which you lock away the money you are willing to lose **before** entering the trade. The term comes from my habit of scribbling the risk amount on a sticky note and physically placing it in a small box on my desk labelled "God Box." Once the note goes in, that money is as good as donated to charity. My job then is not to chase it; my job is to *see* if the market chooses to give me a return gift.

3.5.1 How to Build Your Own God Box Ritual

Decide the rupee risk for your next trade.

Write it down in ink, date it, and sign it.

Fold the paper and put it into a designated container.

Tell yourself aloud: "This money no longer belongs to me. If the trade works, God returns it with interest; if not, so be it."

After market close, if the trade wins, remove the note and tear it. If it loses, transfer the exact sum to a charity jar or a savings account labelled "Tuition Fees."

3.5.2 Why the Ritual Works

Forces explicit risk acknowledgment.

Breaks the brain's attachment to the capital.

Turns loss into a neutral or even positive act (tuition or charity).

Limits revenge trading—you already paid the fee; move on.

I have known traders who replaced the physical box with a digital note or a spreadsheet. That is perfectly fine. The key is to externalise the risk decision *before* pressing the Buy/Sell button.

3.6 Risk-to-Reward Ratio: Quality Over Quantity

A trade with a 1:3 risk-to-reward ratio means you stand to gain three rupees for every rupee you risk. Combine that with even 40 % win rate and you are profitable:

10 trades

4 winners @ +₹3 = +₹12

6 losers @ –₹1 = –₹6

Net = +₹6

Notice how the maths takes the emotional edge off the winning percentage. You don't need to be right all the time; you need to be right *well* when you are right.

3.6.1 Setting Realistic Targets in Options

Options move quickly, but remember time decay. My thumb rule on intraday Bank Nifty options:

Risk: 20-25 points in premium

Target: 40-60 points

Trail aggressively beyond 50 points

This often yields a real-world 1:2 or 1:2.5 risk-reward after slippage.

3.7 A Full Case Study: Bank Nifty Call Trade

Let me walk you through a recent real trade using everything we have discussed.

3.7.1 Background

Date: Thursday, monthly expiry minus one week.Instrument: Bank Nifty 44700 CE.Account size: ₹5 00 000.Daily risk limit (God Box): ₹4 000 (less than 1 %).

3.7.2 Pre-Market Prep

Zone Analysis – Identified 44650 as strong support from the previous two sessions.

Bias – Mildly bullish if price held above 44650 for 15 minutes after open.

Plan – Buy 44700 CE if 5-minute candle closes above first 15-minute high; SL below 15-minute low. Target: 100 points, Trail after +50.

3.7.3 Execution

09:30 a.m.: First 15-minute range forms 44680-44760.

09:35 a.m.: 5-minute candle closes at 44785; buy signal.

Entry price: ₹205 premium.

Hard SL: ₹165 (40-point risk). Risk per lot = ₹40 × 25 = ₹1 000.

Lots allowed: ₹4 000 / ₹1 000 = 4.

Placed market order for 4 lots; simultaneous stop-loss order at ₹165.

3.7.4 Management

09:50 a.m.: Premium hits ₹235. Move SL to ₹205 (break-even). God Box money is now safe.

10:05 a.m.: Premium reaches ₹255. Move SL to ₹225 (lock 20-point gain).

10:20 a.m.: Sudden spike to ₹300. Move SL to ₹275.

10:45 a.m.: Premium wobbles, hits ₹275 and stops out.

3.7.5 Result

Sell price: ₹275Gross gain per lot: ₹70 × 25 = ₹1 750Total gain: ₹1 750 × 4 = ₹7 000Risked: ₹4 000R-Multiple: +1.75R

Notice the modest *number* of rupees risked, the mechanical trailing, and the one-trade-a-day discipline. Rinse and repeat.

3.8 Avoiding Black-Swan Blows: Portfolio Level Risk

So far we talked trade-level risk. Let's zoom out.

3.8.1 Maximum Daily Drawdown

Set a rule: if you lose X % (say 2 %) in a single day, you stop trading. The market may be off rhythm; come back tomorrow.

3.8.2 Weekly Measurement

At week's end, review:

Total trades, win rate, average R, emotional notes.

If a three-day losing streak arises, reduce size by 50 % for next week.

3.8.3 Event Risk

Days with major RBI policy, Fed meet, or election exit polls? Either skip or cut size to 25 %. Volatility can double your planned risk.

3.9 The Psychology Behind Numbers

Numbers are easy; emotions are not. Here's where risk management shines.

3.9.1 Fear of Missing Out (FOMO)

The Daily 1 Trade Rule forces you to choose the **best** setup, taming FOMO.

3.9.2 Fear of Giving Back

Trailing SL addresses the anxiety of a green P/L turning red.

3.9.3 Hope and Pray Syndrome

The God Box ritual breaks this by making loss acceptance explicit before entry.

3.10 Practical Checklists

3.10.1 Pre-Trade Risk Checklist

Have I written the risk amount and placed it in the God Box?

Is my trade size within my position-sizing formula?

Have I placed an automated SL?

Does the trade offer at least 1:2 risk-to-reward?

Am I within my Daily 1 Trade quota?

3.10.2 Post-Trade Review

Was the stop-loss respected?

Did I trail correctly or too aggressively?

Was the emotion log (fear, greed, boredom) noted?

Lessons to carry into tomorrow's *single* trade.

3.11 Common Pitfalls and How to Dodge Them

Moving SL farther to avoid getting hit Fix: Treat the first SL as carved in stone.

Doubling down to recover Fix: Accept the God Box loss; no revenge trades.

Ignoring slippage and brokerage Fix: Include them in risk calculation; target slightly wider.

Risk Creep Fix: Set calendar reminders to audit trade sizes monthly.

3.12 Bringing It All Together

Risk management is not a side topic—it is the *engine room* of every profitable trading operation. Your tasks are clear:

Decide a fixed rupee risk or percentage risk model.

Implement the Daily 1 Trade Rule to focus your mind.

Protect entries with hard SL and nurture gains with trailing SL.

Use the God Box Theory to detach emotionally from money at risk.

Track everything through case-study-style journaling.

Master these, and you will discover that consistent results feel almost "boring." That's the highest compliment for a trader.

Looking Forward

Now that your downside is protected, it's time to sharpen your timing edge. In the next chapter we will decode the language of candlesticks so you know exactly *when* to pull the trigger on that single daily trade.

Chapter 3
Decoding Candlestick Patterns for Market Signals

Introduction – From Shield to Sword

In the last chapter, you and I spent a fair bit of time talking about risk—how to defend your capital like a seasoned warrior. Now that we have our shield firmly strapped on, it's time to pick up a sword. That sword, for many professional traders (myself included), is the candlestick chart.I still remember the first time I truly "saw" a candlestick pattern. It was a lonely Doji that appeared on the daily chart of Reliance Industries back in 2010. One tiny bar signaled exhaustion in a five-day rally, and within forty-eight hours, the market dropped nearly 3 %. I wasn't positioned to profit, but watching that single candle change the narrative flipped a switch in my brain. Price, it seemed, could talk—if only I learned to speak its language.That's exactly what we'll do in this chapter: learn the alphabet, vocabulary, and grammar of candlesticks so you can listen to the market's whispers and, sometimes, its shouts.

---

1. Anatomy of a Candlestick – Reading a Market's Pulse

Before you run scans or count patterns, you need to understand what each candlestick is telling you.

• Open – The first price traded in the chosen timeframe.•. • Close – The last price traded in that timeframe.• High – The highest price reached.• Low – The lowest price reached.• Body – The distance between open and close; its color shows direction.• Wick (or Shadow) – Lines above and below the body showing intraperiod extremes.

Think of the body as the heart, pumping information about who's in control—buyers or sellers. Wicks are the market's extremities, revealing how far each side was willing to stretch before balance returned.

1.1 Time Frames: Why thc Same Candle Tells Different Stories

A five-minute Hammer on Bank Nifty can be noise, while the same pattern on a weekly chart might precede a multi-percent reversal. Match your candlestick analysis to the timeframe you actually trade. Intraday scalpers live inside five- and fifteen-minute candles; positional traders rely on daily and weekly bars. Consistency prevents information overload.

---

2. The Psychology Behind Every Candle

Candlesticks compress the tug-of-war between bulls and bears into a single, easy-to-digest icon. When you spot a long lower wick, you're witnessing sellers push price down only to have buyers refuse that discount and yank the market back.That's not just data—that's drama. Interpreting it accurately comes from visualizing the emotions behind the price. Fear shows up as panic selling (long red bodies), greed as chasing (long green bodies), indecision as short bodies with long wicks.

---

3. Single-Bar Signals – The Market's One-Word Sentences

These patterns involve only one candlestick, yet they often carry surprising weight.

3.1 Doji – Equality or Exhaustion?

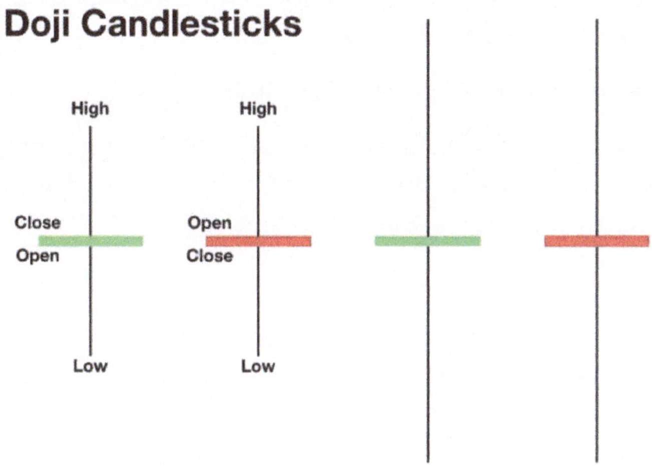

A Doji forms when the open and close are virtually identical. To me, it's the market's ellipsis—"Hmm, not sure." In a long trend, a Doji can herald a pause or reversal. But context is king; a Doji inside a tight consolidation is just noise.

3.2 Hammer and Hanging Man – Same Shape, Different Fate

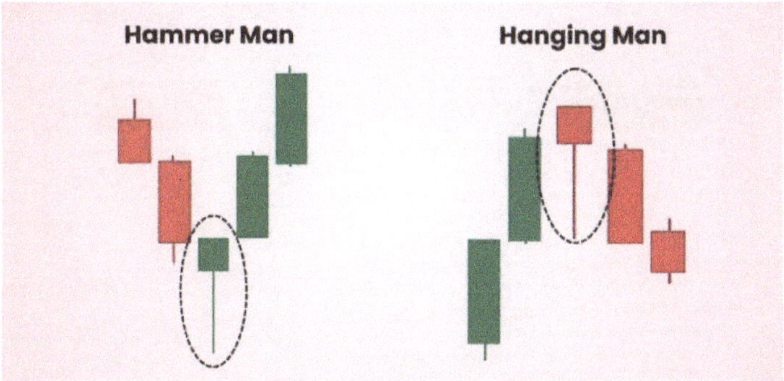

Created by a small body on top of a long lower wick.• In a downtrend → Hammer = potential bullish reversal.• In an uptrend → Hanging

Man = potential bearish reversal.Remember the time Reliance hammered out a low at ₹930 in April 2018? A Hammer on the daily chart coincided with weekly support—within a month, the stock was at ₹1,020.

3.3 Shooting Star and Inverted Hammer

The bearish twin of a Hammer is the Shooting Star (upper wick). If you see one after a steep rise on Bank Nifty weekly, tighten stops. The Inverted Hammer, found at bottoms, suggests bulls are testing contr

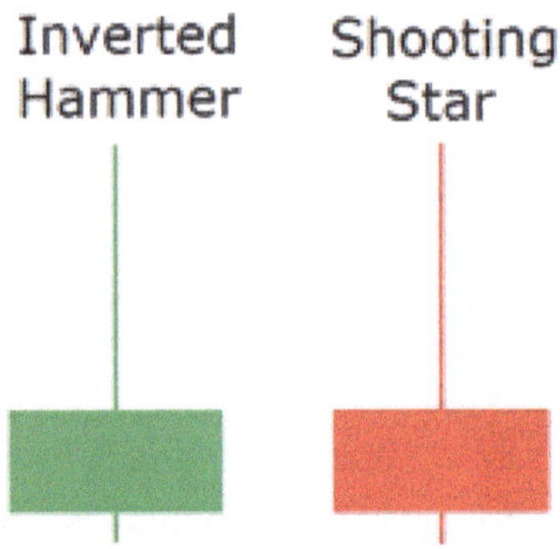

3.5 Spinning Top – Market Shrugs

A small body with wicks on both ends signals low conviction. Useful mostly when it interrupts an emotional streak of Marubozu candles.

4. Two-Candle Patterns – The Market's Dialogues

Now let's add a response candle, turning one-word sentences into short conversations.

4.1 Bullish and Bearish Engulfing

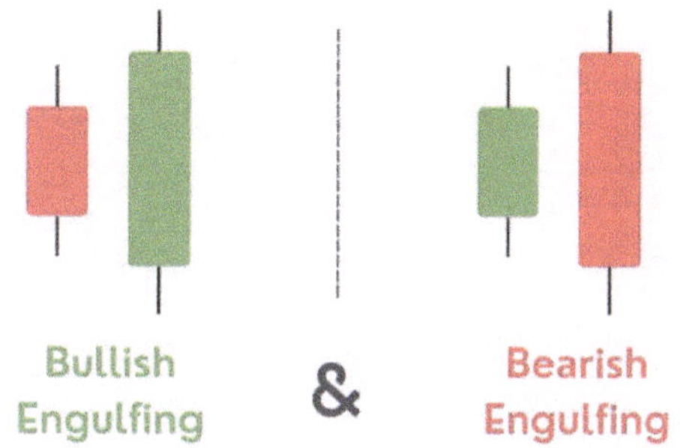

The second candle's body swallows the first. On Nifty IT in May 2020, a Bullish Engulfing off pandemic lows flagged a monster rally.Checklist:• Must appear after a decent trend.• Higher volume increases reliability.• The engulfing candle should close near its extreme.

4.2 Harami – Child in Parent's Lap

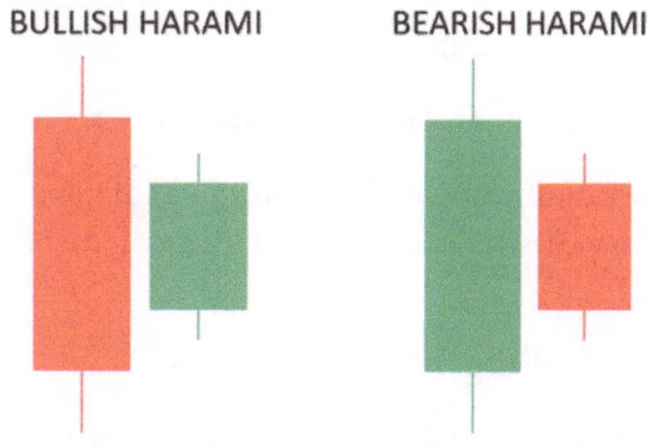

A small body is completely inside the previous large body. A Harami screams "pause." Directional bias depends on trend direction and the breakout of the Harami's range.

5. Three-Candle Patterns – Full Stories

The more bars, the deeper the narrative.

5.1 Morning Star & Evening Star

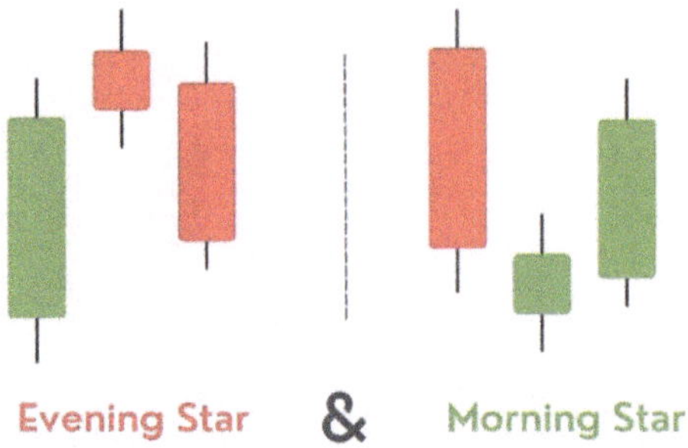

In simple terms, a morning star pattern indicates a buy signal, while an evening star pattern indicates a sell signal. Moreover, there are certain details to factor in before setting up a trade based on either of these patterns. Concerning the morning star pattern, a trader confirms its presence on day three.

5.2 Three White Soldiers & Three Black Crows

A series of three strong closes in the same direction. They often kick off or confirm significant trends. Volume confirmation is crucial—thin volume can spawn traps.

5.3 Three Inside Up & Three Inside Down

Begins with an Engulfing but adds a third candle that breaks the first candle's high (or low). The extra candle offers proof of follow-through.

5.4 Rising and Falling Three Methods

A trend pauses with small counter-trend candles, then resumes forcibly. Use it to pyramid positions, but never forget the "Risk" chapter: raise stops.

8. Building Your Candlestick Playbook

You don’t need every pattern—just a handful that suits your style.

Step 1: Pick 3–5 patterns that naturally jump out at you.Step 2: Back-test them on your preferred time frame and instrument.Step 3: Document entry, stop, and exit rules.Step 4: Rehearse in a demo or micro-lot size for one month.Step 5: Scale only after achieving >55 % win rate and a positive expectancy.

My personal playbook for intraday Bank Nifty options:• Morning Star at 30-minute support.• Bearish Engulfing near VWAP after a gap-up.• Marubozu breakout of opening range.

---

9. Common Mistakes and How to Avoid Them

• Pattern hunting without trend context.• Ignoring volume—the market’s lie detector.• Forcing trades every time a candle looks familiar.• Setting stops too tight below/above wick extremes, getting whipsawed.• Forgetting news catalysts (earnings, RBI policy, Fed talks) that can override technicals.

---

10. Exercises – Train Your Eye

Scroll through the last six months of daily Bank Nifty charts. Mark every Engulfing pattern that occurs near a 20-EMA. Note follow-through in percentage terms.

Print three charts of your favorite stock. Cover the right half, and try labeling potential patterns on the left. Reveal the rest to see accuracy.

Combine a Hammer with RSI divergence on at least five historical setups; track success rate.

---

11. Candlesticks and Options – Timing the Greeks

Because this book focuses on option trading, let's bridge the gap. Candlestick patterns can:

• Improve delta timing: Enter when directional edge peaks.• Aid theta decay: Place credit spreads after Shooting Stars in range markets.• Control implied volatility (IV): A Doji before earnings suggests traders expect calm—selling straddles could exploit later IV crush.

Conclusion – Preparing for the Bigger Picture

Candlestick analysis turns raw price into an intelligible story, helping you spot supply-demand shifts before the crowd. Yet remember, a candle is just one building block. In the next chapter, we'll zoom out to full-blown chart patterns—Head and Shoulders, Triangles, Flags—that frame entire movements. You'll see how single candles combine into structures that deliver some of the market's most reliable opportunities. Let's keep sharpening that sword

Chapter 4
Chart Patterns: Recognizing Opportunities

Introduction – From Candles to Bigger Pictures

In the last chapter, we explored candlestick patterns—those single-bar or multi-bar formations that whisper clues about immediate price action. Now, let's zoom out a little. Instead of focusing on a handful of candles, we are going to stitch dozens, sometimes hundreds, of candles together and look for larger-scale pictures that repeat over and over again. These pictures are called chart patterns, and once you train your eye to see them, they become a reliable compass pointing toward high-probability trades.

When I first started trading, I was obsessed with one-minute candles. I thought the faster the chart, the quicker I'd make money. It took me a string of losses (and a mentor's tough love) to realize that stepping back and spotting the "forest" matters far more than scrutinizing each "tree." Chart patterns helped me make that mental shift from frantic scalper to patient hunter—and they can do the same for you.

What Exactly Are Chart Patterns?

A chart pattern is a recognizable geometric shape formed by price movement on a chart. These shapes tell us two things:

The psychology of market participants (fear, greed, indecision).

The path of least resistance (likely future direction once the pattern completes).

Think of chart patterns as footprints left by big money. When institutions are accumulating or distributing positions, they can't hide the telltale signs. Patterns capture those signs, translate them into visual cues, and give retail traders like us a fighting chance.

The Psychology Behind Every Pattern

Before memorizing shapes, you must internalize the mindset that produces them:

• **Accumulation** – Smart money quietly buying from impatient sellers; price flattens or grinds higher in a controlled fashion.• **Distribution** – Institutions selling to late buyers; price stalls or forms a topping pattern.• **Consolidation** – A truce between bulls and bears; energy coils up for an explosive move.• **Breakout/Breakdown** – The truce ends; one side overpowers the other and price surges or dives.

Whenever you identify a pattern, pause and ask: "Who's trapped? Who's in control? Who will feel pain if price moves one more tick?" The answer often telegraphs the breakout direction.

Reversal vs. Continuation Patterns

Broadly, chart patterns fall into two buckets:

Reversal Patterns – Signal that the prior trend is about to change direction.

Continuation Patterns – Indicate that the current trend is taking a breather before resuming.

We'll tackle each group in depth, but keep this rule of thumb in mind:Reversal patterns usually form after extended, often emotional trends. Continuation patterns form during healthy, orderly trends that periodically pause.

PART I – REVERSAL PATTERNS

1. Head and Shoulders (H&S)

You won't walk into a trading room without hearing about the Head and Shoulders. Picture three peaks: the middle one (the head) taller than the two flanking shoulders.

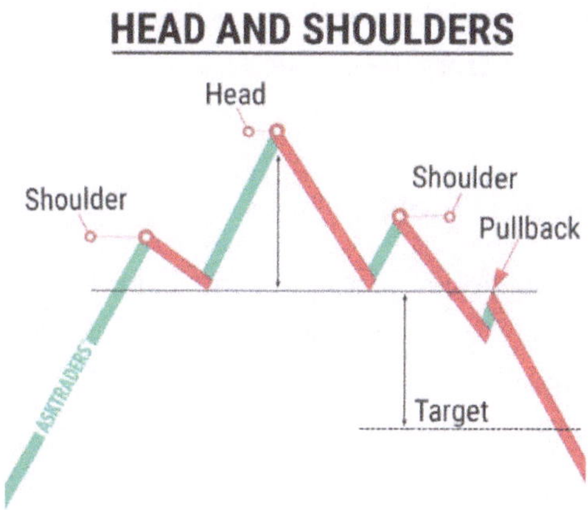

Key Features• Established uptrend preceding the H&S.• Left shoulder forms on rising volume, followed by a pullback.• Head spikes to a higher high, often on lower volume—hinting at waning enthusiasm.• Right shoulder rallies but stalls below the head's peak.• The neckline connects lows between the shoulders and the head; once price closes below it, the pattern triggers.

Measuring Target Distance from head to neckline = X. Subtract X from the neckline breakout point to project the minimum downside.

My Trade Example In: In March 2021, Bank Nifty printed a textbook H&S on the daily chart. After a 28% rally in six weeks, the index formed the left shoulder at 35,000, surged to 37,700 for the head, then stalled around 36,200 for the right shoulder. I shorted 35,000 PE once the neckline (34,800) cracked with above-average volume. The measured move pointed to 32,000. I booked 70% of the position at 32,200 and let the rest ride to 31,800—a tidy 3.2× reward versus risk.

---

2. Inverse Head and Shoulders

Flip the H&S upside down. It represents a transition from downtrend to uptrend. Everything else—volume behaviour, neckline breakout, measured move—mirrors the classic H&S.

---

3. Double Top & Double Bottom

Double Top• Two peaks at roughly the same level separated by a trough.• Confirmation occurs when the price closes below the trough.• Volume often heavier on the first peak and lighter on the second, hinting at exhaustion.

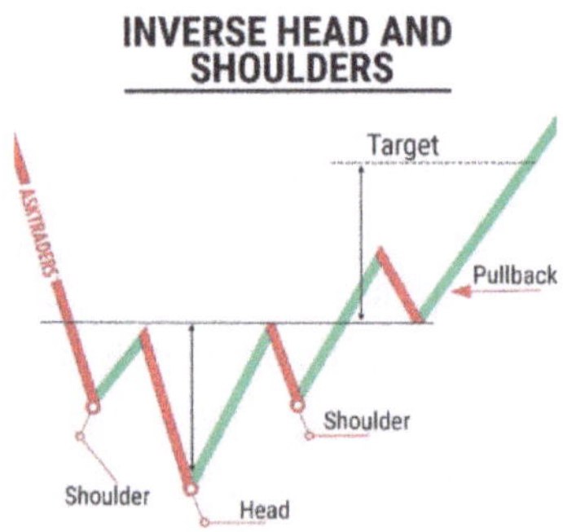

Double Bottom• Two swing lows split by a rally.• Breakout confirms when price closes above the swing high between the lows.

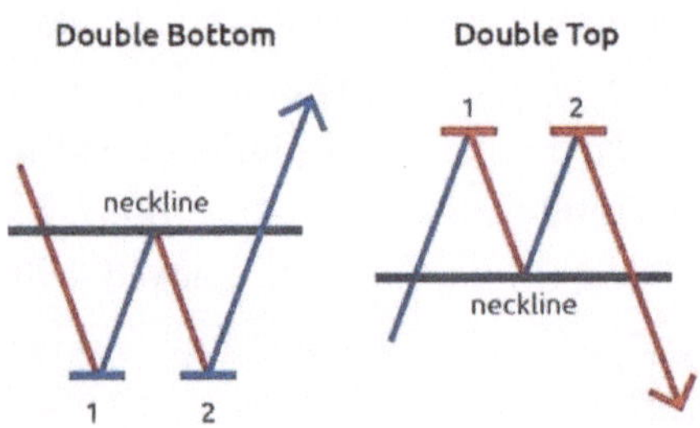

Pro Tip – The distance between peaks (or troughs) and the interim trough (or peak) gives you the price target. Mind the time factor: the two highs/lows must be separated by at least three candles on the timeframe you're trading; otherwise, it's just noise.

---

4. Triple Top & Triple Bottom

A rarer but stronger cousin of the double formation. Three tests of support or resistance wear out the defending side. Once price breaks, the ensuing move often travels farther than most traders expect.

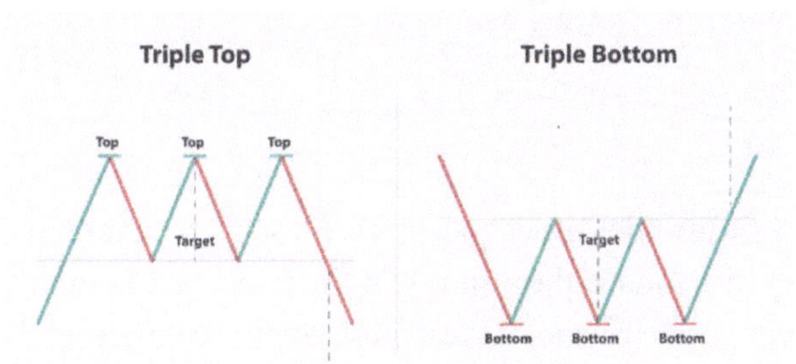

---

5. Rounding Tops & Bottoms

Picture a saucer. The curve tells you buyers (in a top) or sellers (in a bottom) are gradually losing conviction. Volume typically slides during the curve and swells on the breakout. Because these patterns take time to form, they are best spotted on daily or weekly charts.

PART II – CONTINUATION PATTERNS

1. Symmetrical Triangle

Both trendlines converge toward each other, one descending, one ascending. Volume often tapers off, showing consolidation.

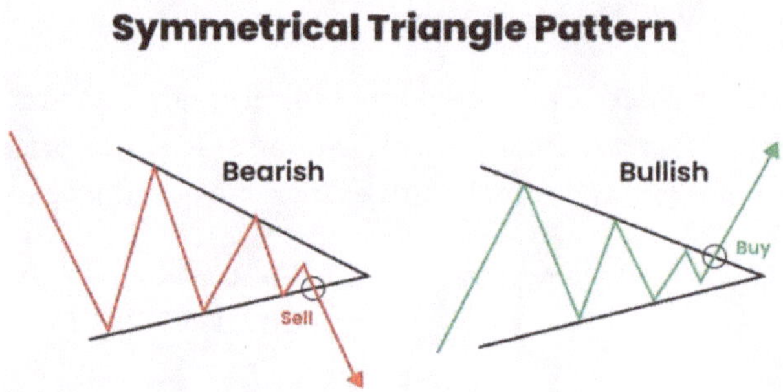

How to Trade• Identify at least five touches (combined on both trendlines) to validate the triangle.• Enter on breakout with volume expansion.• Measure the widest part of the triangle and project it from the breakout point to set a target.

---

2. Ascending & Descending Triangles

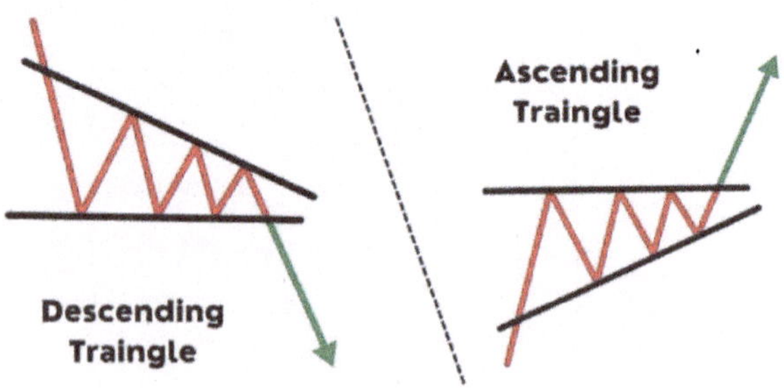

• **Ascending Triangle** – Flat top resistance, rising bottom support. Bias is bullish.• **Descending Triangle** – Flat bottom support, falling top resistance. Bias is bearish.

The logic: one side is repeatedly defending a fixed level; the other side is stepping in at increasingly aggressive prices. Eventually, the persistent bidder (or seller) wins.

---

3. Flags and Pennants

These are my personal favourites for intraday Bank Nifty option trades because they show up after sharp, almost vertical moves. Think of them as a pit stop in a fast race car's journey.

Flag – Small rectangular consolidation that slopes against the prevailing trend.Pennant – Looks like a tiny symmetrical triangle.

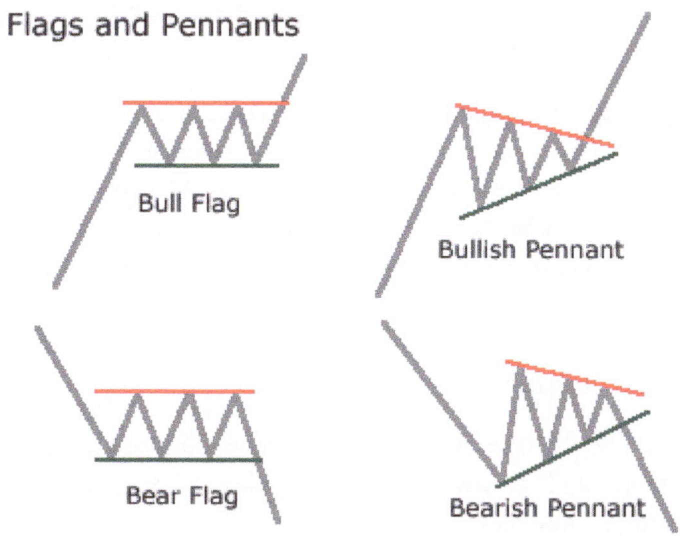

Key traits:•: • Preceded by a "flagpole" (impulsive move on strong volume).• Consolidation is brief—5 to 15 candles on the timeframe you trade.• Breakouts usually occur on a burst of volume; price often travels the length of the flagpole again.

---

4. Rectangles (Price Ranges)

Simple horizontal range where support and resistance are parallel. The longer price coils in a rectangle, the more powerful the eventual breakout.

---

5. Wedges

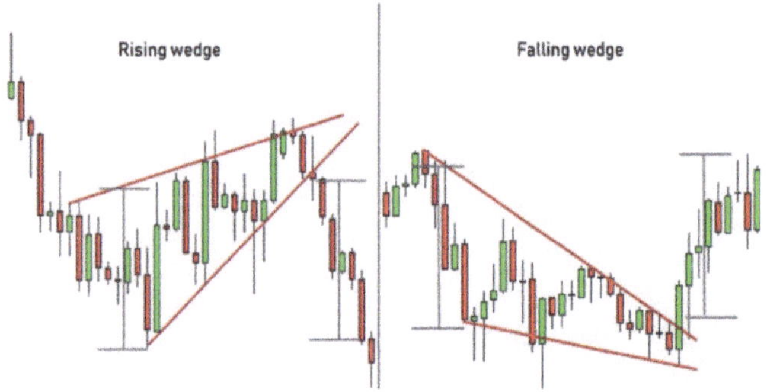

• **Rising Wedge** within an uptrend can be a bearish reversal.• **Falling Wedge** within a downtrend can be a bullish reversal.Within a larger trend, wedges can act as continuations, too. Always pair wedge analysis with volume; contraction of volume inside the wedge plus expansion at the break = higher odds.

---

6. Cup and Handle

Popularized by William O'Neil, it looks like a rounded "U" (the cup) followed by a shallow drift lower (the handle). A breakout above the handle's high completes the pattern.

Ideal Parameters• Cup depth: not more than 30–35% decline from the prior high.• Handle depth: ≤15%.• Volume: Dry up during the handle, surge on breakout.

I love this pattern on weekly charts for swing trades in quality stocks. It marries institutional accumulation with a perfect shake-out of weak hands.

How Reliable Are These Patterns?

No pattern is a magic lamp. Reliability depends on:

• Timeframe (daily > hourly > five-minute).• Preceding trend strength.• Market context (earnings season, macro events).• Volume confirmation.• How clean or "noisy" the formation looks.

On average, reversal patterns have a 60–75% hit rate when properly qualified. Continuation patterns run slightly higher because they align with prevailing momentum. Your job is to stack probabilities: confluence with support/resistance, trendlines (next chapter!), indicators, and sound risk control.

The Importance of Volume

Volume is the lie detector of chart patterns. Here's a quick cheat sheet:

• **Reversal Patterns** – Look for heavy volume on the first peak/trough, lighter on the retest, and a surge on the breakout.• **Continuation Patterns** – Expect declining volume during consolidation and a spike on breakout.

If volume doesn't confirm, tread carefully or reduce position size.

A Step-by-Step Trading Blueprint

Scan charts for one or two clean patterns per session. Don't overdose on opportunities.

Draw trendlines meticulously—wicks count!

Mark the breakout level and pre-calculate entry, stop, and target. I use an R: R threshold of at least 1:2.

Wait for the trigger (close beyond breakout line plus volume surge).

Execute with predetermined position size (see Chapter 3).

Trail stop to breakeven after half the target is achieved.

Book partial profit at measured move; leave a runner if the broader trend aligns.

Log the trade with screenshots—build your personal pattern database.

Common Mistakes To Avoid

• **Jumping the gun** – Entering before confirmation.• **Ignoring volume** – Breakouts on low volume often fake out.• **Forcing symmetry** – If it looks forced, it's not there.• **Neglecting broader trend** – Shorting a small H&S inside a massive weekly uptrend invites pain.• **No stop-loss** – Every pattern can fail; manage the downside first.

Quick Reference Checklist

Before acting on any chart pattern, tick these boxes:

• Trend preceding the pattern?• At least four clean touches on boundaries?• Volume behaving textbook?• Breakout candle close outside pattern?• Risk-reward ≥1:2?• Any major news or earnings ahead?• Confluence with moving averages, RSI divergence, Fibonacci?• Position size aligned with risk plan?

If you score fewer than six yeses, skip the trade.

Conclusion – Patterns Are Maps, Not GPS

Chart patterns offer you a visual map of hidden institutional activity. They enhance your edge, but they are not turn-by-turn GPS navigation. Respect false breakouts, control risk, and keep honing your pattern recognition skills through deliberate screen time.

In the next chapter, we will sharpen our pencils further and learn how to draw and interpret trendlines—the backbone that supports many of the patterns we just covered. Once you master trendlines, spotting and trading these patterns will become second nature. I'll meet you there with a ruler and some real-world examples from my trading journal.

Chapter 6
Mastering Trendlines: Spotting and Riding Trends

What is a Trend Line?

When you start learning to trade you will almost immediately run into a discussion on trend lines. Trend lines are among the most powerful and widely used tools to navigate the markets. They help traders analyze their price chart and identify potential areas of support and resistance, providing valuable insights into the underlying market trends. An understanding of trendlines is crucial for both novice and experienced traders looking to make informed decisions about price action and increase their chances of success.

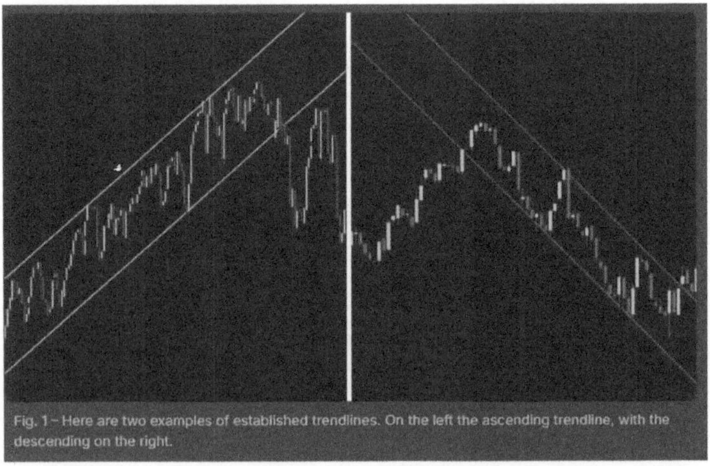

Fig. 1 – Here are two examples of established trendlines. On the left the ascending trendline, with the descending on the right.

A trend line is a core foundational tool that serves as a visual representation of the prevailing market trends. It does this by connecting a series of significant points on a chart and helps determine the presence of a chart pattern. Typically drawn as straight lines, trendlines highlight the direction and the speed of price movements, helping you to identify and understand the underlying market psychology. When we connect peaks or troughs, we use trendlines to establish data points that help with making decisions about buying, selling, or holding a financial instrument. As the price moves along a straight line, these support and resistance levels can provide insights into potential entry and exit points. Lastly, trend lines play an important role in determining false breaks, trend reversals, or continuations, allowing you to anticipate future price actions and adjust your strategies accordingly.

Definition of a Trend Line

A Trend Line is a straight line drawn on a stock chart connecting a series of points to indicate the prevailing price trends of a financial instrument. In more basic terms, trend lines involve connecting a series of prices on a chart to reveal the general direction of stock price movements. This provides a visual representation of the overall trend or the presence of a chart pattern.

Trend Lines can be used for:

Connecting candlestick highs and lows to visualize direction

Assessing market psychology and sentiment to determine potential future price action

Establish potential support and resist levels

Identifying trends on many timeframes and asset types

Determining major shifts in price action behavior

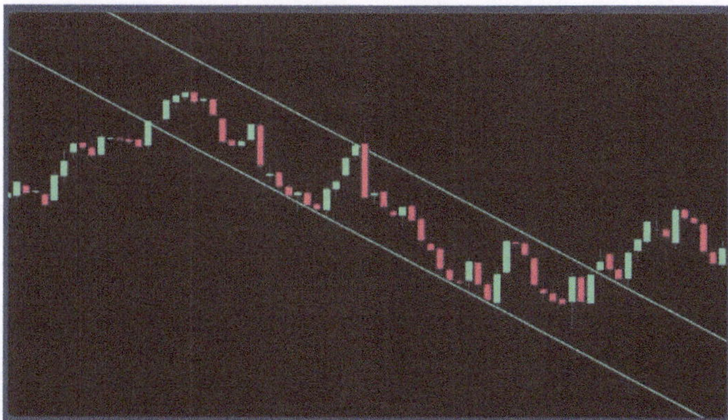

Fig. 2 - This chart shows a descending trendline with strong support. Using a parallel line we can establish the assumed resistance to watch for retests and directional change.

What is a Trend Line in Technical Analysis?

Understanding trend lines in technical analysis is critical for traders as these lines provide valuable insights into the underlying market psychology. By identifying price movement, trend lines help traders identify areas of support and resistance, which are essential in determining potential entry and exit points for their trades. As a core component of technical analysis, trend lines allow traders to monitor price trends on a price chart, anticipate potential trend reversals or continuations, and adjust their strategies accordingly.

Predicting Future Price Movements

Trend lines can be useful in predicting future price movements by providing a visual representation of the market's direction and the prevailing sentiment. By drawing parallel lines, one can identify patterns like an ascending or descending trend channel to anticipate potential trend reversals or continuations. While a linear trendline cannot predict future price chart movements with absolute certainty, they offer a framework for understanding market behavior and gauging the likelihood of certain price actions.

Trendline Support and Resistance Levels

Trend lines help identify support and resist levels by creating a visual representation of the market's overall direction, highlighting areas where the price has historically struggled to move beyond. In an uptrend, the trendline represents a support level, where buyers tend to enter the market, driving prices higher. In a downtrend, however, the trendline serves as a resistance level, where sellers tend to dominate, pushing prices lower.

Assessing Trend Strength

Trendlines are instrumental in assessing trend strength, and more importantly, the likelihood of an existing trend's ability to continue along its trajectory. Linear trendlines reveal the steepness of the trend, which can provide insights into the strength of the underlying bullish or bearish sentiment. A steeper trendline may indicate a strong trend, with higher conviction from market participants, while a flatter trendline may suggest a weaker trend with less conviction, more akin to a typical support and resistance level. Additionally, the number of touches or retests of the trendline can serve as a proxy for trend strength, with more touches often signifying a more robust trend.

Different Types of Trendlines

Trendlines come in various forms and each type provides valuable information for making informed decisions. The three main types of trendlines are horizontal, ascending, and descending. Horizontal trendlines represent a range-bound market, where neither buyers nor sellers have control, and the price oscillates between support and resistance levels. Ascending trendlines, on the other hand, indicate uptrends, where buying pressure pushes prices higher, creating higher lows along the trendline. Descending trendlines signify downtrends, with selling pressure driving prices lower and forming lower highs.

Horizontal Trend Lines

Horizontal trendlines are straight lines representing a range-bound market, where neither buyers nor sellers have clear control. In this environment, the price tends to move sideways between established support and resistance levels. The horizontal trendline is drawn by connecting each significant closing price at either the lows or the highs of the price action. This highlights areas where the price has repeatedly struggled to move beyond. These trendlines provide insights into the market's equilibrium state, where bulls and bears are evenly matched. Traders can capitalize on horizontal trendlines by identifying potential trading opportunities at the support and resistance levels, anticipating price reversals, and employing range-bound trading strategies.

Identifying Range-bound Markets

Trendlines are particularly useful in identifying range-bound markets, where the price moves sideways between established support and resist levels. Horizontal trendlines are drawn by connecting at least two price points, highlighting areas where the price consistently struggles to break through. These trendlines offer traders insights into the market's equilibrium, where neither buyers nor sellers dominate. In the example below we can see that the price action has established and struggled with a very defined range, marked by the horizontal trendlines.

Potential Breakout Levels

Horizontal trendlines also serve as an essential tool for identifying potential breakout levels. These linear trendlines indicate where the price breaks through established support or resistance levels and begins a new trend. By recognizing the horizontal trendline's position to the current market price, traders can anticipate potential breakouts and adjust their strategies accordingly. A breakout above a resistance level may signal a bullish sentiment, indicating a buying opportunity, while a breakdown below a support level may indicate a bearish sentiment, leading to selling opportunities. This trendline data can be used to mark parallel trendlines and help traders identify when a price channel occurs. In the example below we can see the price breaking above an established horizontal trendline, and following through on a breakout.

Ascending Trend Lines

Ascending trend lines are a type of uptrend line that with a positive slope signifies an uptrend, where buying pressure pushes prices higher, creating higher lows along the trendline. We've all heard the chant Higher Lows, Higher Highs! That is another way to think about trendlines. The uptrend lines are drawn by connecting points along the lower end of the chart, highlighting the series of higher lows, which serve as support levels. As the trend line continues to move upward, it serves as a reliable support level for traders to assess potential buying opportunities. Traders can use the ascending trend line to gauge the strength of the uptrend and anticipate potential buying opportunities.

Descending Trendlines

Descending trend lines are a type of negative slope trend line that indicates where selling pressure drives prices lower and creates lower highs along the downtrend line. The negative slope is drawn by connecting price points along the upper end of the chart, highlighting the series of lower highs, which serve as resistance levels. A downtrend line offers traders insights into the market's bearish sentiment. As the trend line continues to move downward, it serves as a reliable resistance trend line for traders to assess potential selling opportunities. Traders can use the descending trend line to gauge the strength of the downtrend and anticipate potential selling opportunities, such as when the price tests the trendline's resistance levels. Selling at or near the trendline's resistance level offers traders an opportunity to enter the market at a higher price and potentially profit from a further move lower along the trend line.

Trend Line Drawing Techniques and Best Practices

Drawing trendlines correctly is important for accurate technical analysis and profitable trading. Trendline drawing techniques and best practices include identifying important price points, selecting the correct timeframe, and using other technical indicators to confirm the trendline's validity. It's important to use a chart that is clear and easy to read, with enough price action to identify highs and lows. When drawing trendlines, traders should connect at least three points on the chart to confirm the trendline's validity and a third point for confirmation. The trendline should then be extended to the right of the chart to identify potential future support or resistance levels. It's also important to periodically re-evaluate trendlines to ensure their accuracy and adjust them as necessary. Traders should use other technical indicators, such as moving averages and oscillators, in conjunction with trendlines to confirm trading decisions and avoid making decisions based solely on trendline analysis.

Conclusion: Mastering Trendlines for Trading Success

In this article we have tried to answer the question "What is a trendline?" and hope we have conveyed that trend lines are a fundamental tool in technical analysis that can help traders identify trends, key levels and potential breakout and breakdown points. While trendlines can provide valuable insights into market dynamics, it is important to use them in conjunction with other technical indicators and to adjust them over time to reflect changing market conditions. Traders should also be aware of the limitations and subjectivity of trendline analysis and be consistent in their approach to avoid common mistakes. By incorporating trendlines into their trading strategies and continually learning and improving, traders can gain an edge in the market and make more informed trading decisions.

Chapter 7
Navigating Support and Resistance Zones

Introduction – From Slanted Lines to Decision-Making Levels

In the last chapter, we dealt with trendlines and learned how those neatly slanted lines can keep us on the right side of a move. But if trendlines are the rails that guide a trend, support and resistance (S&R) zones are the stations where price pauses, refuels, turns back, or even builds up enough steam to break through barriers. When I began trading, I drew what looked like a child's doodle—random horizontal lines everywhere. Some worked, most didn't. What changed everything for me was understanding that those lines weren't just geometry; they represented real money, real emotions, and real liquidity.

In this chapter, I'll walk you through the practical art of identifying, validating, and trading around support and resistance. We'll dig into supply–demand imbalances, FII–DII footprints, liquidity pockets, and the all-important "area of confluence" that you'll hear me repeat like a mantra. By the end, you'll know exactly how to build a map of high-probability price levels and integrate them seamlessly into the 17/18-days profit system we will cement in Chapter 10.

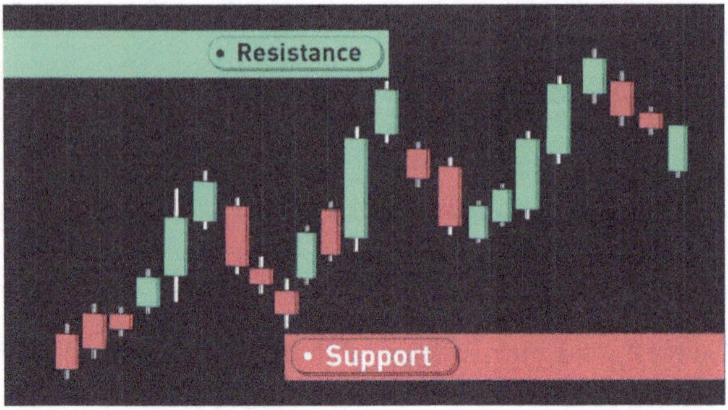

Why Support and Resistance Are the DNA of Price Charts

Before we lay down more lines, let's zoom out and ask a basic question: Why does price stall or reverse at certain levels? The answer lies in the market's DNA: supply and demand.

Every candle is a battle between buyers (demand) and sellers (supply).

Support is the price area where demand overwhelms supply and pushes price up.

Resistance is the area where supply outweighs demand and pushes price down.

When you and I label these areas, we're not predicting the future; we're identifying where history tells us traders were motivated to transact in size. Think of these zones as footprints of collective behavior—fear, greed, profit-taking, and stop-losses all leave clues on the chart.

The Psychology Embedded in a Line

Let's get personal. I once bought Nifty futures during a breakout at 17,850 (back when that felt high). The trade immediately went in my favor by 60 points, but then it stalled and reversed violently from 17,900. I later learned that 17,900 was not just a random figure—it had been a heavy call-writing zone for FIIs, and thousands of retail stops were sitting just above it. That experience hammered home the lesson: each horizontal level is a battlefield of expectations.

When you place a line on a chart, imagine:• There are traders who bought above that line and turned profitable only if the price is higher.• There are sellers who shorted below that line and are nursing paper gains so long as price is lower.• As price revisits that line, those participants decide: hold, exit, or reverse. Their decisions create fresh order flow, which is what you and I want to anticipate.

Key Categories of Support and Resistance

You'll encounter multiple flavors of S&R. Let's quickly catalogue them so you recognize the texture of each.

• Horizontal swing points – Classic daily or weekly highs and lows.• Dynamic S&R – Moving averages, VWAP, Keltner channels that slope with time.• Trendline-derived S&R – Diagonals formed by connecting higher lows or lower highs.• Round numbers – 18,000 on Nifty, 40,000 on Bank Nifty.• Fibonacci retracement levels – 38.2 %, 61.8 %, etc.• Pivot points – Standard, Camarilla, Floor, Woodie—used by day-traders.Our focus in this chapter is on horizontal swing points because they pair best with option strategies in the Indian market, but you'll see how to layer the other types for confluence.

The Birthplace of a Zone – Supply and Demand Mechanics

A zone is different from a single line. Instead of marking 17,850 exactly, you'll draw a band from, say, 17,835 to 17,865. Why? Bodies and wicks fluctuate. Institutions scale in and out, and round numbers act like magnets.

Here is my 3-step method to plot a robust supply or demand zone:

Identify an impulsive move: Look for a sharp, wide-range candle or a series of candles that leave a clear pivot.

Mark the origin: The base of that move is the institution's footprint. That's where the big orders were filled.

Extend the zone: Use the candle bodies for a conservative edge, wicks for aggressive edge.

Case in point: Bank Nifty once rallied 600 points off a base at 41,350–41,450. Every revisit to 41,400 saw aggressive buying for two weeks. That 100-point band became a textbook demand zone.

Liquidity Zones and Stop-Hunts

Liquidity is fuel. Market makers can't move large order blocks unless there's equal willingness on the other side. Hence, price often "wicks" above a well-known resistance or dips below well-known support, taking out stops, before reversing sharply. That wick is not a failure of S&R, it is the stop-hunt that actually validates the zone.

To trade liquidity:• Mark prior highs/lows where retail stops accumulate.• Anticipate a false breakout of 0.25 % to 0.35 % beyond the level.• Wait for a rejection candle or momentum divergence before entering.

Example: On expiry Thursdays, Bank Nifty loves to pierce morning range highs by 100 points, trigger short covers, and then collapse by 300 points. I routinely sell call spreads right after that liquidity grab.

Confluence – The Area of Confidence

A single line is fragile; multiple lines overlapping build a fortress. Confluence happens when two or more independent forms of support or resistance align. My checklist for high-confidence zones:

• Horizontal swing point plus 20-period EMA on the 1-hour chart.• Weekly pivot plus round number.• FII put writing zone plus Fibonacci 61.8 % retracement. When at least two of those align within a 0.3 % band, that's an "area of confidence," meaning I'm willing to size up my trade or tighten my stop.

Common Pitfalls and How to Avoid Them

• Drawing too many lines – Focus on high-time-frame levels.• Ignoring context – A resistance in an uptrend is weaker than in a sideways market.• Blind breakout buying – Wait for confirmation or retest.• Hovering stop-losses – Place stops beyond the zone, not inside it.• No data cross-check – Verify with OI, volume, and market breadth.

Conclusion – From Lines to Edge

Support and resistance are not magic, but when you map them with institutionally influenced supply–demand logic, validate them with FII/DII footprints, and respect liquidity behavior, they morph into a formidable edge. Draw fewer, stronger zones; wait for price to come to you; and you'll find yourself on the right side of the market more often than not.

In the next chapter, we'll add yet another layer of timing precision by introducing trading indicators—moving averages, RSI, MACD, and Bollinger Bands—and learn how to mesh them with the zones you've just mastered. That's where the real synergies begin. See you there!

Chapter 8
Trading Indicators: Enhancing Analysis and Timing

Introduction – From Static Levels to Dynamic Clues

In the previous chapter, you and I spent a good deal of time drawing horizontal lines—learning how support and resistance give us a static framework to understand where the market might react. Those price levels are crucial, but the market is alive and rarely stays still. Candles race up and down, volatility contracts and expands, and new information constantly gets priced in. Static levels alone can't reveal the whole story.

That's when I first turned to technical indicators, back in 2014, after being "wick-hunted" for the tenth time in a month. I realised I needed tools that could move with price, tools that translated raw movement into digestible signals so I could act faster—and with more confidence. Indicators helped me see hidden momentum, subtle shifts in sentiment, and changes in volatility. In this chapter I'll walk you through the handful of indicators that I've battle-tested in Indian markets, show you exactly how I combine them with price action, and warn you about the pitfalls that trap most beginners.

By the end of these pages, you'll be able to:

• Distinguish between trend-following indicators and oscillators• Set up and interpret Exponential Moving Averages (EMAs) for intraday and positional trading• Harness the Relative Strength Index (RSI) to spot momentum shifts and early reversals• Read MACD and Bollinger Bands so they reinforce rather than contradict your analysis• Build an indicator "playbook" you can rely on—in equities, currency, or the ever-volatile Bank Nifty options you'll study in the next chapter

Let's dive in.

---

1. Why Indicators Matter (and Why They Often Don't)

Before we get technical, let's address the elephant in the room: some veteran traders preach "price action only," claiming indicators are lagging junk. The truth sits in the middle. Indicators are merely mathematical transformations of price and volume. By definition, they follow price, so they do lag. But lag isn't necessarily bad. If raw price is like a high-speed train rushing past, indicators are the CCTV cameras slowing down the footage so you can see which door opens first.

Properly used, indicators give three priceless advantages:

Context – They tell you whether current movement is strong or weak relative to recent history.

Timing – They help you wait for confirmation instead of chasing every candle.

Discipline – A rule-based indicator system reduces snap judgements and emotional trading.

Indicators become a crutch only when you pile on so many that the chart resembles Diwali lights. The goal isn't to predict each tick; it's to build a framework for consistently higher-probability decisions.

---

2. My First Encounter with Indicators – The 9 EMA Revelation

Let me share a quick war story. Early in my career I traded Nifty futures with nothing but candlestick patterns. My win-rate was decent, but stops were wide because I feared getting shaken out. One day a mentor asked me to add the 9-period EMA on a five-minute chart.

"Think of it as the market's pulse," he said. "As long as candles close above the pulse, the heart is healthy."

That single line was transformative. I noticed that during strong intraday trends, price would repeatedly kiss the 9 EMA, then sprint away. Instead of guessing bottom or top, I started waiting for price to revisit the EMA and show a bullish or bearish rejection candle. Trade after trade, my entries tightened, and my risk–reward ratio doubled. The indicator wasn't predicting anything; it just quantified the speed and allowed me to hitch a ride without chasing.

Keep that image in mind: indicators are a trader's stethoscope. They amplify subtle beats you might otherwise miss.

---

3. Two Broad Families: Trend-Followers vs Oscillators

Every indicator you'll meet falls into one of two buckets.

• Trend-Following (Lagging) – Moving Averages, MACD lines, SuperTrend, Ichimoku, ADX; they ride trends and keep you on the right side of momentum but trigger late in choppy markets.• Oscillators (Leading) – RSI, Stochastic, CCI, Williams %R; they fluctuate between fixed bands, signalling possible reversals before they happen, but they can stay "overbought" or "oversold" for painfully long periods in trending markets.

Using one family in isolation is asking for trouble. A powerful combo pairs a trend-follower to stay aligned with the primary direction and an oscillator to fine-tune entries and exits. My go-to pair is EMA (trend) + RSI (oscillator), sprinkled with MACD or Bollinger Bands for extra context.

---

4. Moving Averages – The Market's Conveyor Belt

4.1. SMA vs EMA: The Anatomy

A Simple Moving Average (SMA) calculates the arithmetic mean of closing prices over n periods. Every data point is weighted equally. The result is smooth but slow to respond.

An Exponential Moving Average (EMA) assigns more weight to recent prices, reacting faster to new information. This responsiveness makes the EMA my preferred choice for intraday and swing trading in high-beta Indian names like Reliance, Tata Motors, and of course, Bank Nifty.

4.2. The Key EMAs You'll See on My Charts

• 9 EMA – The micro trend. Works brilliantly on 3- to 15-minute charts.• 20 EMA – The short-term trend, also doubles as dynamic support/resistance on hourly or daily timeframes.• 50 EMA – Intermediate trend; institutions track it, making it reliable for positional trades.• 200 EMA – The granddaddy. When price lives above the 200 on daily charts, the market is considered in a primary up-trend.

You don't need all four on every chart. Choose based on your trading horizon. For intraday Bank Nifty options I stick to 9 and 20 EMAs; for positional equity trades I overlay the 20, 50, and 200.

4.3. EMA Crossover Strategy – A Classic with an Indian Twist

A standard system triggers a long trade when the 9 EMA crosses above the 20 EMA and exits (or reverses) when it slips below. It's straightforward, but the Indian derivative market has nuances—gap-ups and gap-downs thanks to overnight global cues. Here's how I filter:

Ignore crossovers that occur within the first 15 minutes of the session—opening volatility skew can generate whipsaws.

Demand at least a 0.5% distance between price and the previous day's close before acting. This rule saves you from chasing gaps that instantly reverse.

Example: On 24 May 2022, Bank Nifty opened 1.2% higher. The 9-20 crossover fired on the first candle, but price was already 400 points from the previous close. I passed. Ten minutes later, the index dropped 300 points, erasing amateur gains while I sipped coffee.

4.4. Dynamic Support & Resistance – Riding the EMA Wave

Picture a surfer. The wave's slope tells him when to paddle harder, when to stand, and when to bail. Trend-following traders can treat a rising 20 EMA as that wave. When price repeatedly tests and respects the EMA, the trend is healthy. Once price cuts through and the EMA flattens, the wave is dying.

Here's a simple protocol I use:

• Three or more touches of the 20 EMA in a clear up-trend strengthen the level.• A candle closing 0.3% beneath the 20 EMA (with volume expansion) is my first warning to tighten stops.• A follow-through lower close confirms the trend has shifted—time to exit longs or flip short.

I'll show you this visually in the case studies later.

---

5. Relative Strength Index (RSI) – Reading the Market's Muscle

5.1. The Core Formula, Minus the Maths Headache

RSI, created by J. Welles Wilder, compares the magnitude of recent gains to recent losses over a look-back period (default 14). The output oscillates between 0 and 100:

• Above 70 – traditionally “overbought”• Below 30 – traditionally “oversold”

But if you merely buy at 30 and sell at 70, you’ll bleed. Trends can push RSI to 80 or higher and stay there for days. So we need deeper insights.

5.2. RSI Ranges – Bullish vs Bearish Behaviour

In healthy up-trends, RSI tends to oscillate between 40 and 80, rarely dipping below 40. In down-trends, it lives between 20 and 60. Memorise this:

• RSI floor at 40 = bullish range• RSI ceiling at 60 = bearish range

When RSI breaks its usual range, expect a trend change. I use this concept religiously on the 15-minute chart of Bank Nifty. If after a steady morning up-move the RSI bottoms at 42 instead of the usual 30, I know bulls still have fuel.

5.3. Failure Swings – Catching Reversals Early

A bullish failure swing happens when RSI dips below 30, rises above 30, pulls back but holds above 30, then breaks the prior high. This four-step pattern often precedes a price reversal before divergence is visible.

Mark these steps on paper until it becomes muscle memory. I once snagged a 700-point intraday Bank Nifty rally on 12 July 2021 purely because of a textbook bullish failure swing—price looked bearish but RSI told a different story.

5.4. Divergence – The Early Canary

• Bullish divergence: Price makes a lower low, RSI makes a higher low.• Bearish divergence: Price makes a higher high, RSI makes a lower high.

Divergence is powerful on higher timeframes (hourly, daily) but can be a minefield on 1-minute charts. When trading weekly options—

where theta decay punishes hesitation—I double-check divergence on two timeframes (say, 5-minute and 15-minute) before committing.

5.5. Custom Settings for Indian Markets

While 14 is the global default, I prefer:

• RSI 9 for intraday scalping—more sensitive, perfect for Bank Nifty's turbo moves.• RSI 21 on daily charts—provides a smoother signal for positional trades and syncs with the monthly F&O expiry cycle.

Test both on your preferred instruments. Remember, an indicator's value is proportional to how many market participants watch the same setting. That's why I rarely go below RSI 9—too few traders track a 5-period RSI, making signals unreliable.

• Identify a trend via EMA or MACD.• Enter on a minor pullback that stays above the middle band in an up-trend (or below in a down-trend).• Trail stops a candle beyond the opposite band or at a fixed ATR value.

---

8. Marrying Indicators with Price Action – The Confluence Edge

Indicators don't replace candlesticks, trendlines, or horizontal levels; they complement them. My highest-probability trades tick at least three boxes:

Structure – Support/resistance or pattern breakout.

Trend Alignment – EMA direction or MACD histogram.

Momentum Confirmation – RSI range or Bollinger expansion.

For instance, if price bounces off a daily support zone (structure), the 20 EMA slopes upward (trend), and RSI prints a bullish failure swing (momentum), the odds stack heavily in my favour.

Avoid analysis paralysis. More than three indicators usually dilute, not add. Remember, confluence means different data points pointing to the same conclusion, not the same indicator on multiple timeframes.

---

12. Common Indicator Mistakes and How to Avoid Them

• Indicator Overload – Limit yourself to one trend-follower and one oscillator plus maybe a volatility tool.• Chasing Overbought/Oversold – In strong trends, "overbought" is a feature, not a sell signal.• Ignoring Higher-Timeframe Bias – A 5-minute bearish divergence means little if the daily chart is in a fresh breakout.• Curve Fitting – Tweaking settings until the past looks perfect guarantees future disappointment. Stick to common parameters unless data prove otherwise.• Disregarding Event Risk – RBI policy days will blow up textbook setups. Stand aside or trade reduced size.

14. Tools and Platforms for Indicator-Driven Trading in India

• TradingView – Clean charting, social scripts; downside: limited broker integration for Indian F&O.• Zerodha Kite – Lightweight, reliable, offers basic EMA, RSI, MACD, Bollinger; no advanced back-tester.• Amibroker – Steep learning curve but unparalleled for custom scans. I use it for bulk back-tests on NSE Bhavcopy data.• Sensibull – Options platform that overlays Greek data; their "Positions" tab helps track delta when you combine indicator signals with option strategies.• Excel/Google Sheets – Old school but gold. I pull daily OHLC into Sheets via GOOGLEFINANCE and compute custom EMAs for weekend analysis.

Choose a platform that feels intuitive; shiny features are useless if you hesitate during live trades.

Conclusion – Indicators as Your Trading Co-Pilots

We've journeyed from understanding why indicators matter to dissecting the nuts and bolts of EMAs, RSI, MACD, and Bollinger Bands. You now know how to blend them with price action, avoid common traps, and codify them into a repeatable playbook. Indicators won't guarantee profits—nothing does—but they'll sharpen your timing, instil discipline, and reduce emotional noise.

In the next chapter, we zoom into the Bank Nifty index itself—the beast that magnifies both risk and reward. You'll see how its composition and volatility statistics mesh perfectly with the indicator framework you just learned, enabling you to craft strategies tailored for India's most exciting trading instrument. Ready? Let's unlock the secrets of Bank Nifty.

Chapter 9
The Bank Nifty Index: Structure, Volatility, and Trading Strategies

A Quick Look Back—From Indicators to Indices

You and I have just finished exploring the universe of technical indicators—those trusty companions that give an extra layer of confirmation to price action. Now let's zoom in on the instrument that, for thousands of Indian options traders, is the daily playground: the Bank Nifty index. If candlesticks are the alphabet and indicators the grammar, Bank Nifty is that best-selling novel everybody's talking about. Understanding its plot twists, characters, and recurring themes can level-up your trading in ways no textbook definition ever could.

---

1. What Exactly Is Bank Nifty?

1.1 Origin and Purpose

Launched in 2003 by NSE Indices (formerly IISL), the Nifty Bank index—colloquially "Bank Nifty"—was designed to track the performance of the most liquid and large-capitalization banking stocks listed on the National Stock Exchange of India (NSE). The motivation was simple: banks drive credit, credit drives growth, and growth defines India's economic pulse.

1.2 Current Composition and Weighting

As of this writing, Bank Nifty is a free-float market-capitalization-weighted index of twelve banking giants. The exact constituents may shuffle during periodic reviews, yet you'll almost always find a mix of:

• Public-sector behemoths (State Bank of India)• Private-sector leaders (HDFC Bank, ICICI Bank, Axis Bank, Kotak Mahindra Bank)• High-beta corporate lenders (IndusInd Bank, Bandhan Bank)• Niche or turnaround stories (AU Small Finance Bank)

Weightings fluctuate daily with market cap, but historically the top four private-sector banks command roughly 60–65 percent of the index.

1.3 Contract Specifications You Should Memorize

• Lot size: 35 units (revised periodically; always verify on NSE circulars)• Tick size: ₹0.05• Weekly expiry: Every Thursday (or previous working day if a holiday)• Monthly expiry: Last Thursday of the month• Strike interval: ₹100 or ₹200 (depending on spot level)• Trading hours: 9:15 a.m. to 3:30 p.m. IST

Why memorize these? Because one overlooked detail—like forgetting a weekly expiry holiday—can invalidate an otherwise perfect setup.

---

2. Anatomy of Bank Nifty Volatility

Bank Nifty's personality is best described as mercurial. It yawns for hours and then bolts like Usain Bolt. Recognizing what fuels those sprints separates the amateurs from the pros.

2.1 Event-Driven Catalysts

RBI Policy Meets: The Monetary Policy Committee (MPC) decisions often reprice interest-rate expectations within seconds.

Quarterly Earnings: A single NPA-related line item can move an entire banking pack.

Global Bond Yields: U.S. 10-year spikes translate into instant fear for emerging-market banks.

Liquidity Updates: CRR/SLR tweaks, LTRO announcements, and government borrowing plans.

2.2 Intraday Rhythms

• The 9:15–9:30 "amateur hour" whipsaw.• A 12:00–12:30 lull as traders wait for European cues.• A 2:30–3:15 power move, often aligning with institutional rollovers.

2.3 Statistical Measures You Should Track

• Implied Volatility (IV): Available on NSE option chain; above 30 percent signals possible straddle plays.• Historical Volatility (HV): Look at 10-day, 20-day windows. When IV dwarfs HV, premium selling becomes lucrative.• ATR (Average True Range): Daily ATR divided by spot gives you a percentage sense of typical range.

4. Reading Order Flow and Market Breadth

Order flow can feel like reading Matrix code, but three lenses make it digestible.

Open Interest (OI) Profile: Rising OI with rising price = aggressive longs. Falling OI with rising price = short cover rally.

PCR (Put-Call Ratio): Below 0.8 suggests excessive calls; above 1.3, puts dominate. Extreme values often precede reversals.

Bank vs. Fin-Nifty Divergence: If Fin-Nifty underperforms by >0.75 percent, be skeptical of Bank Nifty rallies.

Case Study—28 October 2021 Weekly Expiry: A PCR of 1.5 alongside a falling spot tipped me to a sudden put-short squeeze that netted 120 points in 15 minutes.

---

5. Seasonality Hacks: Knowing the Calendar

You wouldn't surf without checking tides; why trade Bank Nifty without its seasonality map?

• April–May: Fiscal-year results. Elevated IV, straddle firms thrive.• June–July: Monsoon progress; PSU Banks react to rural credit chatter.• September: Global risk off? Historically weak for Indian banks—bear call spreads shine.• November–December: Festive credit demand; momentum trend-following suits.• Union Budget (Feb): Expect three-sigma moves. Trade long gamma or stay flat.

---

6. Building a Bank Nifty Playbook

A playbook distills chaos into checklist items. My personal playbook pages look like this:

Macro Snapshot: USD/INR, US 10-year yield, SGX Nifty pre-open levels.

News Scan: RBI notifications, PSU bank recap headlines, global banking stress alerts.

Technical Layout: Daily trendline slope, 20-EMA alignment, previous session's VWAP.

Option Metrics: IV percentile, OI heat map, max pain shift.

Trade Candidate: Strategy + entry, exit, max loss, max target.

Psychology Cue: "I will exit if the thesis is invalidated; not when P&L hurts."

Remember, the goal is to automate good behavior, not just trade execution.

---

7. Risk Management Specific to Bank Nifty

Bank Nifty's average intraday range (usually 1.8–2.2 percent) is bigger than Nifty50's. That bigger canvas needs thicker guardrails.

• Position Sizing: Risk no more than 1 percent of capital per Bank Nifty trade.• Time-Based Stops: If my premise hasn't played out by

2:45 p.m., I punch out—theta decay becomes my enemy.• Max Daily Drawdown: 3 percent. Once hit, the system locks me out.• Hedging: Long volatility edges (buying wings) are non-negotiable in event-driven markets.

---

8. The Psychology of Trading a High-Beta Index

Bank Nifty amplifies not only price movements but emotions. Expect adrenaline spikes matched only by skydiving—minus the parachute if you're unmanaged.

• Confirmation Bias Trap: Believing every green tick reinforces your bullish thesis. Solution: Pre-define invalidation points.• Revenge Trading: One failed straddle doesn't demand an immediate re-entry. Walk away.• Overtrading: Volatility lures action junkies. Keep a hard cap on trades/day—three for me.

Mind Hack: I keep a sticky note— "BANKNIFTY IS NOT YOUR THERAPIST"—right on my monitor. It reminds me that the index won't fix my mood; only disciplined execution will.

---

9. Technology Stack—Tools I Personally Use

Broker: Discount broker with a reliable API.

Scanners: Streak or TradingView scripts for IV percentile and OI shifts.

Execution Automation: Python AutoTrader for predefined SL orders.

Journaling: Edgewonk or simple Google Sheets to tag trades—strategy, mood, outcome.

Backup Internet: Mobile hotspot; Bank Nifty won't pause because my Wi-Fi does.

Tip: Test every tool in simulation during two full expiries before going live. A software glitch at 3 p.m. Thursday can erase a week's gains within seconds.

---

10. Putting It All Together—Sample Month-Long Plan

Week 1 (Post-Expiry Fresh Series)• Bias: Directional; trend often establishes.• Strategy: Debit spreads or naked directional futures with tight SL.

Week 2• Bias: Mean-reversion as early euphoria cools.• Strategy: OTM credit spreads; watch ATR contraction.

Week 3 (Earnings + Event Cluster)• Bias: Vol expansion.• Strategy: Long gamma—straddles, strangles.

Week 4 (Expiry)• Bias: Premium decay.• Strategy: Iron condors, iron flies, calendar spreads.

Adjust for anomalies: RBI policies or global crises reset the template—always flexible.

---

11. Common Pitfalls and How to Dodge Them

• Ignoring Lot Size Changes: NSE revises; wrong size skews risk.• Over-leveraging on Expiry Day: Easy to think "small stop-loss." Remember: slippage widens.• Misreading OI Shifts: A change near 2:45 p.m. could be option writers closing, not fresh positions.• Trading During

Illiquid Spreads: Deep OTM wings can have ₹5–10 spread; use limit orders.

Case Study—20 May 2022: A friend punched market orders on deep OTM hedges, paid ₹12 higher than LTP, erasing half the iron fly edge.

---

12. Advanced Tactics for Professionals

If you've mastered basics, consider these next-level angles.

Delta-Neutral Intraday Scalping: Continuously rebalance futures vs. option deltas to harvest gamma.

IV Skew Arbitrage: Monitor weekly vs. monthly IV. When weekly becomes unusually rich, short weekly and long monthly.

Statistical Pairs: Trade Bank Nifty against PSU Bank index when divergence hits historical extremes.

---

14. Checklist Before Every Bank Nifty Trade

☐ Global cues checked (Dow futures, Asian markets)☐ Domestic news scanned (RBI, Finance Ministry)☐ Volatility environment identified (IV Rank)☐ Strategy matched to volatility (Buy or Sell premium)☐ Stop-loss and target defined☐ Position size ≤ 1 percent capital☐ Contingency internet/back-up power ready☐ Trade journal entry created pre-trade

Complete it, or skip the trade. Simple.

---

15. Conclusion—Why Bank Nifty Deserves a Spot in Your Arsenal

Bank Nifty is not just another ticker; it's a condensed barometer of India's financial ecosystem—liquid, volatile, option-rich, and event-laden. For disciplined traders, it offers unparalleled opportunities to rack up those 17–18 green days each month that we'll engineer systematically in the next chapter. For gamblers, it's a catapult straight into the red.The choice, as always, is yours. Equip yourself with the structure, respect the volatility, apply the strategies, and you'll find that the "difficult" Bank Nifty suddenly becomes the most predictable member of your trading watch-list.

Smooth Transition to Chapter 10

Now that you and I speak Bank Nifty's language fluently, it's time to design an entire month-long regimen—the 17/18 Days Profit System. In the next chapter, we'll weave together everything you've learned so far—risk management, candlesticks, indicators, and today's Bank Nifty insights—into a step-by-step blueprint you can start executing from the very next trading session. See you on the profit side!

Chapter 10
Designing the 17/18 Days Profit System in 22 Trading Days

It's about to break. Okay. Now, let's start this chapter, and before we begin, I'll outline some points that we will discuss in this chapter. This is going to be the most important chapter because this is where your entire setup will be ready, and you'll learn how to make a profit in seventeen to eighteen days out of twenty-two trading days. Moving on to this chapter, I'll explain some points and rules for trading this setup, so pay close attention. First, backtest it for ten days, then trade with real money for thirty days using one or two lots, and then continue. You'll see that your portfolio will never be in the red; it will always stay green.

In this chapter, the first point we'll discuss is

1. **how to select the strike price**. The strike price is a very important aspect, so we'll talk about how to select it in detail.
2. **The second thing we'll discuss is how to draw the liquidity** zone in Bank Nifty. We'll go through the step-by-step process of drawing the liquidity zone.
3. **After that, in the third point, we'll talk about how to set the Lawrence setup** for Nifty and Bank Nifty.
4. **Premium chart setting for banknifty**
5. **Then, in the fourth point, we'll discuss confirmation**. We don't take any trade randomly; we take trades after seeing some confirmation, so we'll talk about how we decide on confirmation.

Then, we'll combine all four or five elements, and based on the highest confirmation, we'll execute the trade.

There's a rule for this: **the one trade rule daily.** Understand that you should only make one trade per day. Do not make more than one trade, even by mistake. The timing for trading will be from 9:15 to 10:00 in the morning in Bank Nifty. After that, do not make any trades. Follow the one trade rule daily for thirty days, and even after these thirty days, continue it for a lifetime. This is risk management that you need to follow.

Those with small capital should start with one lot, and those with larger capital should start with two lots. But I would prefer you to start with two lots. Consider trading as a business. If you open a business, it requires an investment of 40,00,0, so think of this as investing in a business, and you only need to invest once and rotate it. Start with two lots. When it comes to stop loss, our minimum stop loss is 25 points. If the stop loss is 25 points, it doesn't mean you should take a 100-point stop loss. You can take 30 or 35, but if you're taking 100 points, that's your mistake.

Keep a ledger for everything. Make a journal of everything. Write down every trade you make, whether you took a call or a put, at what price, where you exited, and where you entered. I'll also attach a ledger here to show you how to make one. Follow the ledger and manage your trades accordingly. Do this for thirty days, and then for the next thirty days, continue managing your trades like this. Only by following this risk management will you be able to succeed.

How to select the strike price.

In this topic, we are going to discuss how to select the strike price. This topic is very important. What you have learned before was basic. You can find all that on YouTube and in many books. But from here on, what we will discuss is not something you will find on YouTube or in any books. This is all my practical knowledge. And from here, how will you make a profit in seventeen to eighteen days? In twenty-two trading days, I am going to declare the entire roadmap. So, start making notes from the books here and read each thing repeatedly to gain more knowledge on it.

The first point we have here is how to select the strike price. You see, the biggest problem that everyone from beginners to experienced traders faces is which strike price to select, and the second thing, which index to trade? So, guys, I will answer both of these in this chapter. After this, I will explain everything in detail as we move forward.

So, how to select the strike price? Everyone has their own theory. My theory is a bit different. And if you focus on one thing, you can achieve it much faster. For the last six years, I have been following one index, which is Bank Nifty, and I have dedicated all my time to it. That's why today I can catch every move in Bank Nifty.

First of all, I am not going to talk about ATM, OTM, ITM, etc. I will talk about how to select the Strike price in a simple way with the help of Delta. Now, what is Delta? I have already explained Delta in previous chapters, but I will give a brief overview. What is Delta? Delta is an option Greek that tells you how much the premium point will move if the spot price moves by a hundred or two hundred points. Based on this, we select the type.

For example, let's say the Delta of a strike price call is 0.60. You bought the call from there. Now, if the spot price moves a hundred points, and the Delta of that strike price was 0.60, how much profit will you make? Not a hundred points. You have to multiply it by the movement. This is automatic multiplication. So, you should keep in mind that 0.60 multiplied by a hundred means your profit is sixty rupees or sixty points. This is how you can calculate Delta.

If we take the daily Delta, I focus on Bank Nifty, so I will first explain Bank Nifty. Currently, the monthly expiry is ongoing, and it changes over time. Sometimes it's weekly, sometimes it's monthly. That's up to SEBI. But if I take it in context now, I am considering the monthly expiry. So, if I talk about the monthly expiry, note down when not to trade or select. First, the Bank Nifty expiry is mostly on the 28th of every month, between the 28th and 30th of the last month. So, you should not trade for two to three days before the expiry because the premium is very high at that time. Let the premium adjust for two to three days. Let the market settle a bit. After that, you can trade.

Now, how will you select the strike price after two to three days? Simply, you need to set up a chart in the option chain, with calls on one side and puts on the other. You can check out the figure below to see how I have set up calls on one side and puts on the other. Now, you need to look for a Delta between 0.40 and 0.60 for both calls and puts, and select that strike price.

Many people have theories about this. If you select a strike price with a Delta of 0.40, and the market moves a hundred points, you will make a profit of forty points if you bought the call. Many people have the theory that if the movement is less, the profit will be less if your Delta is low. If your Delta is high, the profit will be high. But if the Delta is high, the premium will also be high. For example, if you check the premium of a Delta of 0.40, it might be four hundred rupees, and for a Delta of 0.60, it might be six hundred fifty rupees. Everyone's capital is different; some trade with less capital, some with more. So, I have come up with a universal thumb rule that the Delta between 0.40 and 0.60 for both calls and puts should be selected. That's it. Simple. Look at the figure below. I have selected and placed it accordingly.

The Biggest Question—Why Bank Nifty?

Now, I'll talk about this topic in a bit more detail because everyone asks me why I trade Bank Nifty. Why don't I look at any other index or stock? So, guys, let me tell you something simple: it's better to focus your mind on one thing rather than running it in seven different directions. This way, you can concentrate better. That's what I've been doing for the last six years—only observing the movements of Bank Nifty. I analyze the Bank Nifty chart every morning. When the market closes in the evening, I look at Bank Nifty again. Because of this, I've developed such a strong grasp on Bank Nifty that, while I won't claim to capture its movements 100%, I can capture about 90%

of them. That's why I use Bank Nifty, whether it's to take its premium or to trade.

My theory is that you should focus on keeping your monthly portfolio in the green. It doesn't matter which index you're trading in, which stock, whether it's forex or crypto. It doesn't matter to me, and it shouldn't matter to you either. What should matter to you is keeping your portfolio green every month. That's why you should start trading in Bank Nifty too. Focus on it, look at its chart, and you'll start catching its movements within 1 to 2 months. You'll start understanding it. It took me 6 years, but it won't take you 6 years. It might take 60 days because I didn't have a mentor to guide me back then. But now, you have this book, which is going to be a huge asset. In the future, this book will be life-changing for everyone because it will provide you with complete knowledge.

That's why I always keep Bank Nifty in my arsenal, trade in it, and select its premium. I select the premium from the call side on one side and the put side on the other. I apply all the charts and indicators to Bank Nifty and follow them. So, that was the question of why I trade Bank Nifty. Now, how will we step by step apply Bank Nifty to the chart? I'll explain all of this as we progress through this chapter. Because in this chapter, I'll provide you with a complete roadmap on how to make a profit in seventeen to eighteen days and keep your portfolio 100% to 200% green in a month if you trade by following the rules.

Okay, let's move forward in this chapter, and after this, we'll come to the date liquidity zone.

How to draw the liquidity zone in Bank Nifty

Now, let's talk about what the liquidity zone, which can also be called the area of confluence, or another name I've given it is the FII and DII zone. What is this? Let me discuss it point by point. There are certain steps to find out the liquidity zone. By following these steps, you can create a daily liquidity zone and keep it on your chart. This will be your hidden chart. On one laptop, the front chart will be the premium chart for call and put options. Then, on one side, there will be the Lorez chart, which we will discuss later. What is Lorenz, how to use it, and all that. And the hidden chart will be the liquidity zone chart, which is the most important chart.

Now, what do we look at to create this liquidity zone, and what steps do we follow? Let me discuss those steps. Okay, so first of all, guys, we are going to talk about finding the liquidity zone in Bank Nifty. Now, let's assume we have to trade tomorrow. The market has closed today, so we need to find the liquidity for tomorrow's trade. The first step is step number one. What you need to do is set the timeframe to one day. After setting the timeframe to one day, mark the swing high and swing low from the last three months' data. You can look at the downside fair and set the swing high and swing low accordingly. What you need to do is draw a horizontal line extending forward. The second point is that when you set the swing high, it's not necessary to set multiple lines if the market has gone up and down from a single price point multiple times. You can approximate and set a single line there. This will simplify things for you. So, create a range accordingly. Mark a line at every place where you set the swing high and swing low. Extend the horizontal line forward. This is step number one.

Now, move on to step number two. What do you need to do here? You need to shorten the timeframe. Set the timeframe to two hours. After setting the timeframe to two hours, mark the swing high and swing low from the last forty-five days' data. Just like you did in step one, do the same thing in step two, but keep the timeframe for forty-five days. Now, keep the color of the horizontal line a little different. This will give you an idea of which one is for one day and which one is for two hours. After marking this, look at the downside chart; it will look like this.

Now, come to step number three, which is the most important step. Why is this the most important step? Because, as you know, FIIs and DIIs buy and sell in the market daily. Big traders, mutual fund managers, and banks buy and sell daily. So, to know their position, step number three is very important. What do you need to do for this? Mark the previous day's open price, high price, low price, and close price for the next day. Mark these four points, these four lines, for the next day. After marking this, you will have a total of six lines: one day, two hours, open, high, low, close. Now, shorten the timeframe to five minutes or 15 minutes, whichever timeframe you trade in. Mostly, set it to 15 minutes and leave it.

Now, how will you trade on this? If you see that in any price range, which is called a price range, for example, if I talk about Bank Nifty, from 51,200 to 51,300, this 100-point price range is a price range. So, if you see that in any price range, if two or more than two lines that you drew earlier fall within a range of fifty to a hundred points, then what will it be? It will be an area of confidence, or you can call it a liquidity zone. The more lines, the stronger the area. Remember, the more lines, the stronger the area. So, if you see two lines in a price range below, four lines in another, and three lines in another, what will it be? It will be the market's liquidity zone.

Now, how do we form our view on this? Look, the chart of the liquidity zone you use is to form a view of whether the market is bullish or bearish in a larger timeframe. So, if the market is above a liquidity zone, you need to hold off on trading until the market touches a liquidity zone. Suppose the market comes down from above and touches a liquidity zone. In that case, you will see how many zones are there. If there is the previous day's low or high, there should be more than two zones, which will act as strong support. The reverse is true if the market is going up or there is some resistance above, like the previous day's low or a one-day line or a two-hour line; there should be two lines. This will create resistance. This creates an area of confidence.

Now, let's look at how we determine the total number of confirmations. The first confirmation we consider is the one-day horizontal line. The green line you see here represents the one-day line, while the other green line represents the two-hour line. The most important elements we focus on are the previous day's high, previous day's low, and previous day's closing price.

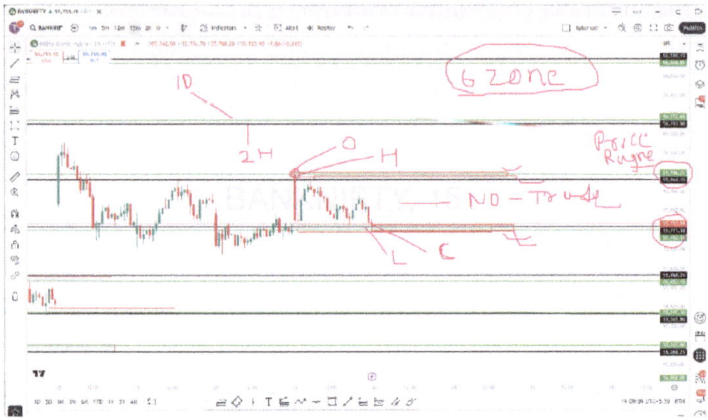

If you look at the chart below, you can see where the market opened. The previous day's open, high, low, and close are the four key points we need to mark for the next day. For example, in the chart, you can see the market's open price, the previous day's low, and where the market opened and closed. Based on this, we draw these levels forward to create a box or range for the next day.

When we analyze the total confirmations, we observe that there are six zones in total. These six zones include the one-day line, the two-hour line, and the open, high, low, and close levels. Together, these form six zones.

Now, how do we initiate a trade based on these zones? The more zones that exist within a price range, the stronger that price range becomes. This is the price range you can see circled in the chart. If a price range contains two or more zones, it becomes a high-liquidity zone. The more zones within a price range, the stronger the zone and the higher the liquidity in that area.

Based on this, if the market is above the liquidity zone and there is a strong zone below with 3-4 zones, we can plan a bullish trade when the market approaches that zone. Conversely, if the market is below the liquidity zone and moving upward toward a strong liquidity zone, we can plan a bearish trade. However, if the market remains within the liquidity zone, this is considered a no-trade zone. In such cases, we do not plan any trades.

Here, we discussed the six zones and how they provide confirmation. Sometimes, the market may only have two or three zones, and in such cases, we adjust our confirmation accordingly. However, we do not rely solely on the liquidity zone chart to take trades. Instead, we use it to form a view of whether the market is likely to be bullish, bearish, or sideways. These zones are strong because large traders often use higher timeframes, which is why we take confirmation from liquidity zones. But to actually take a trade, we set up a premium chart.

In the next chapter, I will explain the Lauren setup in detail. After that, I will provide more insights and show how we incorporate it into the premium chart.

So, how will you plan on this? You can keep it as a side chart or a hidden chart to see your view of the market's form and position. If the market is coming down from above near a liquidity zone, the liquidity zone will be our first confirmation for a call side or long position. If it's coming down from above, and if the market is going up from below and touching a liquidity zone above, what will our view be? It will be bearish, for the put side or short position. So, you can draw the liquidity zone accordingly. I am attaching some photos for you. By looking at them, you will get a complete idea.

After this, we will talk about the Lorenz setup. We will combine everything together. Right now, I am telling you step by step what we need to put on the chart and how we will trade with confirmation. In the end, we will mix everything together and then initiate the trade. So, you need to put the liquidity zone on the hidden chart. After this, we will move on to step number two, directly to the Lorenz chart, and how to set up the Lorenz chart.

loren setup: a game changer setup

in this topic, we are going to discuss the Loren Setup, the magical setup. This setup is very special to me because I designed it in 2020. We will have a full discussion about this topic. However, many people who are reading the book might not have the Lawrence Setup. I will explain in the book how to get this setup and for those who already have it, how to continue using it.

So, first of all, what is the Lawrence Setup? I created this setup in 2020. How did I make this setup? I am also a Pine Script coder. So, what did I do? I mixed five or six indicators to create a Pine Script and named it the Lawrence Pankaj Setup.

Now, what is the purpose of this setup? What I am going to talk about is how to make a profit in 17 to 18 days, and we will do it through Lawrence. We will do intraday trading and scalping with it. For that, using Lawrence is very important. Having Lawrence is crucial. Since the time I started writing this book, I designed it four years ago, and I have kept my portfolio mostly green by using it, and more than 10,000 people are also using it. So, understand that this setup was a life-changer and a game-changer for me, and I hope it will be a life-changer for you too if you follow its rules.

In the Lawrence Setup, two things are very important: one is its EMA, which is automatic, and the other is its trendline, which is also automatic. We are going to talk about these two things, and we take confirmation from them.

Now, you can see in the figure below. The Lawrence Setup is applied to this chart. On one side, there is a Nifty chart, and on the other side, there is a Bank Nifty chart. Both have Lawrence applied, and the time frame for both is five minutes.

Now, what are the components of Lawrence? The EMA you see, if you want to get Lawrence, I am providing a link here. You can copy and paste this link into Google to get Lawrence, apply it, or if you want to trade without Lawrence, what should you do? Apply a 14

EMA with the setting HL-C3 on both charts, and you will have to mark the trade line yourself. How to mark the trade line? I have already explained in the previous chapter that you have to mark the trade line by touching three points.

So, in a five-minute time frame, your Lawrence chart will be applied to Nifty and Bank Nifty. Applying the Lawrence chart is very important because this is where we start taking confirmation. We mainly look at two things: one is the EMA, and the other is the automatic trade line that forms. I have already mentioned that if you have Lawrence, you don't need to apply this EMA or trade line. But for those who don't have Lawrence, apply the 14 EMA on both charts with the setting HL-C3, keep both on a five-minute time frame, and these two charts will be in front of you. This will be the Lawrence Setup.

How to Set the Premium Chart

How do you set up the premium chart? Because the money that is made comes from the premium chart itself. I have already explained how to select the strike page in a previous chapter, so if you're wondering how to choose the strike page, that has already been discussed. Now, in this chapter, we will talk about what settings need to be applied to the chart.

First of all, if you look at the figure below, you'll see two charts displayed side by side. On one side, there's the call chart, and on the other side, there's the put chart. From here, you can check the details for both call and put, including their respective timings. In this chapter, we will discuss this in detail.

The time frame for these charts will be as follows: one side will display the call chart, and the other side will display the put chart. Both charts will have a one-minute time frame. Now, let's talk about the EMA (Exponential Moving Average) settings. You can see this in the call chart. I will also share a screenshot of the EMA settings with you. You can check the screenshot below to see the EMA settings. These settings need to be applied to both charts, which will remain on a one-minute time frame for both call and put.

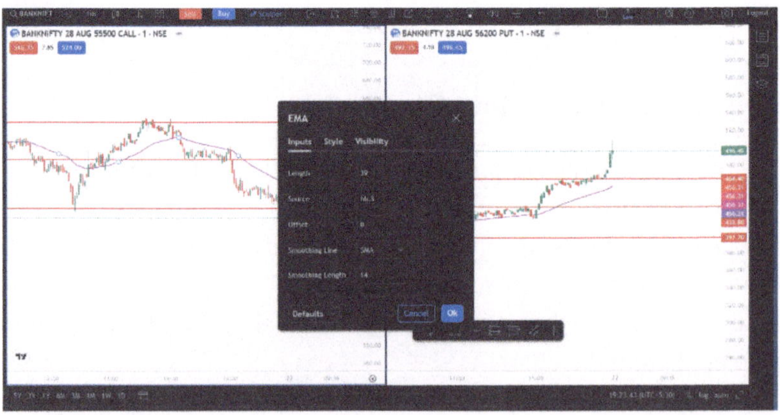

This will be your primary chart, from which you will initiate your trades. Remember, the money is made in the premium chart, so it's essential to set this up properly.

Now, what will this setup help you with? First, it will give you clarity on the entry level, stop loss, and exit level. As soon as the market opens, how do we confirm our trades?

The first confirmation comes from the EMA. The EMA serves as our initial confirmation. After that, you need to look at the previous day's high and low levels. These include the open, low, high, and close of the previous day, as well as the swing high and swing low.

If you look at the figure below, you'll see the swing high and swing low marked. What you need to do is draw horizontal lines at these swing high and swing low levels. This will help you determine your entry and exit targets.

In the chart, I have drawn multiple lines, which you can see below. These lines represent the previous high and low levels. Using these, we can plan our entries.

So, the chart setup will include two confirmations:

1. The EMA, which provides the first confirmation.

2. The previous swing high and swing low, which add another layer of confirmation for entry, stop loss, and target levels.

In the next chapter, we will discuss how to take trades after analyzing all these confirmations. The more confirmations you have, the more confident your trades will be. In the next chapter, we will cover all the confirmations in detail and discuss how to execute trades based on them.

Confirmation and taking a trade

In this topic, we will discuss confirmation. We never place any trade randomly. Before taking any trade, we always check for confirmation. The more confirmations a trade has—whether on the call or put side—the more confident the trade will be. This also increases the chances of the market moving in our favor, resulting in higher accuracy.

Based on this, let's review the confirmations we've discussed so far. I'll summarize them point by point for clarity.

The first confirmation we checked was in the liquidity zone. This was based on the one-day time frame's horizontal zone, which we created using swing highs and swing lows. This is the first confirmation.

The second confirmation was the horizontal line in the liquidity zone on the two-hour time frame.

The third was the previous day's open.

The fourth was the previous day's high.

The fifth was the previous day's low.

The sixth was the previous day's close.

These six confirmations make up the liquidity zone confirmations.

Now, let's move on to Lorin confirmations. In Lorin confirmations, we check two things:

1. The EMA (Exponential Moving Average) for Nifty and Bank Nifty.

2. The automatic trendline that is generated.

These two confirmations are added here. Those who have access to Lorin will trade using Lorin's charts. For those who don't have Lorin, you can click on the website link provided below to get details. https://t.me/pankajsahuofficial

In the premium chart confirmations, the first confirmation is the 39 EMA for both call and put trades. Additionally, we mark the previous day's high and low, which are created using swing highs and swing lows. These also serve as confirmations.

In the premium chart confirmations, the swing highs and swing lows that are marked help us determine the entry point, stop-loss (SL), and target.

In total, we have 11 confirmations. Now, let's assume you are entering a trade. If that trade has more than 2 or 3 confirmations, it will be considered a high-confirmation trade. On the other hand, if the market provides only 2 or 3 confirmations, it will be considered a low-confirmation trade.

Remember, the more confirmations a trade has, the higher its accuracy. If a trade has 7-8 confirmations for either the call or put side, it becomes even stronger.

I will show you some examples to help you understand how to determine entry points, stop-loss, targets, and confirmations. I will also display some figures to illustrate this in detail

Now look at the example below. As you can see, I've circled a section in the figure on the downside. If you observe closely, what confirmations are visible near the circle in the market? We can see four confirmations. What are these four confirmations?

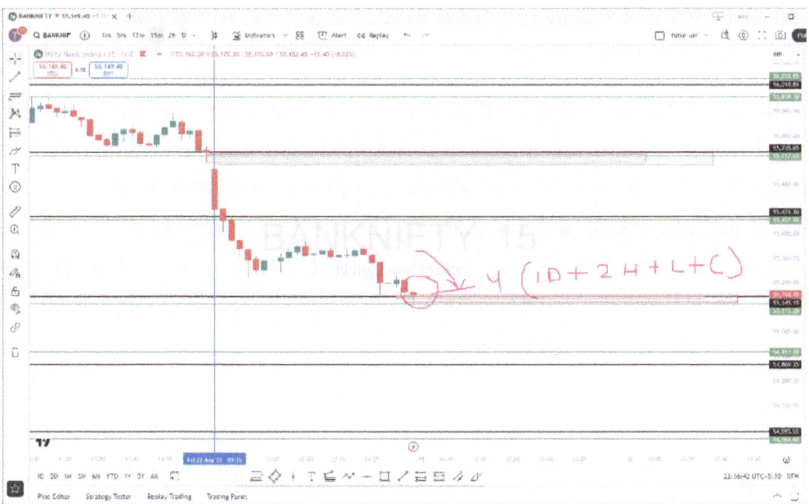

Take a look: there's a red line, which means one day; there's a black line, which means two hours; plus the previous day's low; and the previous day's close. At this price point, we can see four confirmations. So, if the market stays above this price point and approaches it, what will our plan be? It will be on the call side. However, we don't make entry or exit decisions solely based on liquidity zone confirmation. Our main strategy determines our entry, exit, and overall plan.

The liquidity zone helps us form a view. If the market is near the liquidity zone and there are 2-3 confirmations, we then check the premium chart and trade based on those confirmations. Here, I can see four confirmations. Now, look at another figure below. We've identified four confirmations for a trade. Follow the chart of Lorin below.

This chart is for Nifty and Bank Nifty. Here, I mentioned that we follow two confirmations: one is the trade line, which you can see marked with an arrow, and the other is the EMA. This also adds confirmation. So, let's assume that the market is near the liquidity zone, moving upward, and approaching the liquidity zone. Here, I can see the EMA and the trade line. Now, two more confirmations are added, making it a total of six confirmations.

Since we have a total of 11 confirmations, if we get 6 or 5 confirmations, sometimes it may happen that only the EMA or the trade line is visible. Many people might ask why the Nifty chart is included alongside the Bank Nifty chart. The components of Bank Nifty, such as HDFC, ICICI, and SBI, are also part of Nifty. That's why we follow the Nifty chart as well. However, our primary focus remains on the Bank Nifty chart.

If I see that the market is moving away from the liquidity zone and I notice an EMA and a trade line, as marked in the figure, the EMA and trade line create support. Based on this, our plan will be on the call side. So far, it should be clear that the market is approaching the liquidity zone, and I can see that the market is above the EMA and the trade line. If the market enters this range, we move to entry, stop-loss (SL), and target in the premium chart.

Now, look at the premium chart below. On one side, there's a call, and on the other side, there's a put. You can see this. Since our view from above, based on the liquidity zone and Lawrence setup, indicates a call-side movement, we decide on entry, SL, and target in this premium chart. This is based on a one-minute time frame.

Here, we mainly follow the previous day's high, low, swing high, swing low, and the same day's high and low. You can see these marked with red lines, which represent the previous day's highs and lows. The EMA and red lines also act as support and resistance or help determine entry, SL, and target. The EMA, marked with an arrow, plays a key role.

Let's assume we see a bullish move, and the market is below the EMA in the premium chart. How do we decide the entry point? When the market breaks out above the EMA, we can determine the entry point above the EMA. The stop-loss can be set at the red line marked in the figure.

How do we decide the target? The red lines marking swing highs and lows will be our targets. Based on these lines, you can set the first target, second target, and third target. Starting from the liquidity zone and moving to the Lawrence setup, your view of the market will become clear—whether the movement is on the call side or the put side. Based on this, you can make your entry.

For example, if the market is below the liquidity zone and there's heavy liquidity above, your view will be bearish. Then, you'll draw all the lines for the put chart—entry, SL, and target. You can also note down some points from the premium chart. Let me explain a few points about entry.

The red line you see can also act as an entry point. Sometimes, the market may remain above the EMA without retesting it. In such cases, the first target I've marked at 482 can be your entry point. The red line and EMA will help decide your entry and target.

What are the do's and don'ts? I'll discuss these in the next topic and explain everything. Based on this approach, you can create one trade daily. The trade will be solid, and the more confirmations you have, the better your trade execution will be.

Do’s and Don'ts

In this, I will discuss what you should and shouldn’t do in options trading. We will cover everything in detail. But always remember one thing: whatever I’ve explained to you so far, don’t invest your money until you’ve observed the market yourself for at least thirty days. First, practice paper trading. Watch the market, learn, and understand it thoroughly. Only then should you trade with real money.

Now, coming to the dos and don’ts, the first point to always remember is that if the market opens with a gap-up or gap-down of 300 to 350 points in Bank Nifty, you should avoid trading on that day.

Second, you should plan your trades between 9:15 AM and 10:00 AM. This 45-minute window after the market opens is when you should strategize your trade.

Third, follow the "one trade per day" rule. Never take more than one trade in a single day. If you take more than one trade, you are breaking the rule.

Now, let’s say the market opens with a gap-up or gap-down of 350 points in Bank Nifty. On such days, you shouldn’t trade. However, there’s a trick for when you can trade in such situations. For instance, if the market gaps up by 350 points but reverses to your level within 10 to 15 minutes, you can plan your trade from there. Take note of this. If the market gaps up or down by more than 350 points, there’s a high chance it will either continue in that trend or move sideways. But if the market reverses within 10 to 15 minutes—whether it drops after a gap-up or rises after a gap-down—you can consider entering a trade at that point. Observe this carefully and follow this rule.

The fourth rule is to always manage your capital. If you’re trading in Bank Nifty, your stop-loss should not exceed 30 to 35 points.

Primarily, you should focus on Bank Nifty. For the first month, spend your time observing the market and the strategies I've explained earlier. From the second month onward, start trading with one lot. Continue this for thirty days.

The fifth rule is to always trail your target. For example, if you've planned your trade and entered it, your fixed stop-loss should be 25 points—no more than that. Your target should follow a 1:1 risk-reward ratio. This means if your stop-loss is 25 points, your target should also be 25 points. If you're trading with one lot, you should book your profit at the first target. If you're trading with two lots, book profit on one lot at the first target (1:1 risk-reward ratio) and trail the stop-loss for the second lot to cost-to-cost (CTC). This means you move your stop-loss to your entry point. Then, hold the second lot for a 1:2 risk-reward ratio. Once the second target is achieved, book your profit and exit. Follow this rule.

Now, the seventh rule is about Bank Nifty's expiry. Bank Nifty expires every month, typically on the 28th, 29th, or 30th. For two to three days after the expiry, you should avoid planning any trades. Why? Because after expiry, fresh premiums come into play, and these premiums are usually very high. This means your capital will be more heavily utilized, and your profits will be lower. Additionally, during these three to four days after expiry, the market often moves sideways, causing the premiums to melt. So, for these three to four days, just observe the market, understand it, and learn from it, but don't plan any trades.

Your goal should be to execute 15 to 16 trades every month. Out of 22 trading days in a month, aim to take 15 to 16 trades. You'll notice that most of these—around 13 to 15 trades—will end up being profitable.

These are some of the dos and don'ts, and there are many more. Follow these rules and execute your trades accordingly. I've seen people who have followed these rules for six, seven, or eight months, and their capital has doubled, tripled, or even quadrupled.

How Operators Trap You

In this topic, we will discuss the various ways in which operators trap retail traders. Trading is not a shortcut to success; it is a discipline that, over the long run, can turn you into a profitable trader. Those who think they can become millionaires in just four or five days, or even a month of trading, are nurturing a major misconception. Operators take full advantage of this mindset.

Statistics show that 90% of traders lose their entire capital within 30 days. How do operators manipulate the market? I will explain this through 5-6 key points. As I've mentioned before, when you observe charts daily, you'll start to understand how operators trap retail traders in the market. Below are some points to notice. These situations don't happen all the time, but they do occur, and it's important to know what to do when they arise.

First, when you see the spot chart moving but the premium is not moving, you should avoid taking a trade at that time. This is a common trap set by operators.

Second, if you notice that the premium is moving but the spot chart is not, you should also refrain from trading in this situation.

Third, there are times when the spot chart is moving upward, forming green candles, and the call premium is increasing, but the put premium is not dropping. In such situations, operators are setting a trap. What happens here is that it appears to retail traders as though both sides are moving, prompting them to enter a trade. However, the operator keeps the put silent and then suddenly moves it, triggering stop-losses for many traders. In such cases, you should avoid trading as well.

Fourth, I've already mentioned the importance of timing. Between 9:15 AM and 10:00 AM, you should focus on conducting a full analysis based on the points I've outlined above. Only after completing your analysis should you execute your trade. If a trade opportunity arises after 10:00 AM, you should not take it. All your analysis and trade execution should be completed before 10:00 AM.

Fifth, follow the one-trade-per-day rule. No matter what happens, you should never take more than one trade in a single day.

By keeping these points in mind and maintaining discipline, you can avoid falling into the traps set by operators and improve your trading outcomes over time.

Must follow golden rule

Every trader chases strategies. But the truth is, strategies alone won't make you rich. The one thing that separates winners from losers in the market is the Fifteen Golden Rules of Trading. If you don't crack these, the market will break you every time. Trading isn't a game; it's a life-changing battlefield. If you step onto this field, you must be prepared—mentally, emotionally, and with discipline. The real game here is about patience and understanding.

Let's begin this journey with the **first Golden Rule**: Never stop learning. The market is new every day, offering fresh lessons daily. If you think you've learned everything, that's where your downfall begins. Charts change every day, trends shift, and human emotions evolve. If you stop learning, you'll get lost in the crowd. Understand that trading is like an ocean with endless waves. To learn how to swim, you must keep learning every single day.

The second rule is to learn how to control your mind. In trading, your biggest enemy isn't the market—it's the impatience within you. You want to make money quickly and see instant results. But the market doesn't give anything instantly. It tests you, challenges you. If you can't manage your mind, the market's swings will throw you off. Patience is your greatest weapon—the art of waiting and the wisdom to act at the right time.

The third rule is to always keep risk under control. The biggest mistake people make is betting without calculation. Never put all your strength into a single trade. Always think, "If this goes wrong, how much will I have left?" This mindset will keep you in the game for the long haul. The trader who wins is the one who plays the field for a long time. If you lose everything quickly, you'll be out. Risk management is your shield.

The fourth rule is that discipline is king. Without discipline, trading is like riding a bicycle without pedals—you won't move forward. You need to set rules for yourself every day: when to enter, when to exit, how much to invest, how much to earn, and how much you're willing to lose. Everything should be decided in advance, and once decided, you must stick to it. Discipline is what sets you apart from the rest.

The fifth rule is to learn to read the market's language. Every chart tells a story, every candlestick sends a message. The market speaks, but few listen. If you learn to listen, the market will show you where the crowd is rushing and where the smart players are preparing to strike. Treat the market like a language—read it like a child reads a book. Slowly, its patterns will become clear to your eyes.

The sixth rule is to keep emotions away from your decisions. Anger, fear, greed, hope, restlessness—these emotions lead to bad decisions. You must stay calm. The market will heat up, people will shout, the screen will flash red and green, but you must remain composed. If you let emotions drive your decisions, they will eat away at your money.

The seventh rule is not veiwing each day in isolation. Look at the bigger picture. Small profits and losses come and go, but you must always calculate where you'll stand in a month, a year, or ten years. This mindset turns a trader into an investor. Don't get upset over small ups and downs—think big and play big.

The eighth rule is to treat trading not as a job but as a lifestyle. If you take it seriously, every decision you make will revolve around how it impacts your trading. Time management, sleep, focus—everything will strengthen your trading. Trading rewards those who make it a habit in life.

The ninth rule is to learn practically, not just from books. Books and courses are good, but the real master is the market itself. Invest money, but start small. Then watch how the market teaches you. Take notes, make mistakes, learn, and correct them. This is real education.

The tenth rule is to never follow the crowd. In the market, when everyone is rushing in one direction, the real opportunities lie where no one is looking. When everyone is buying, stay cautious. When everyone is selling, observe carefully. The crowd leads to losses. Learn to think independently and walk your own path.

The eleventh rule is to start small and grow big. Everyone wants to make millions on the first day, but trading doesn't work that way. Take small steps, make small bets, and enjoy small wins. These small steps eventually open up big opportunities.

The twelfth rule is to stick to your plan. Often, people make plans but abandon them when the market turns. The real player is the one who stands firm on their plan. The market's job is to scare you, and your job is to stick to your rules.

The thirteenth rule is to invest in learning. Not just in stocks and options, but in yourself. Invest in books, courses, tools. Invest in your mind every day. This investment will yield the greatest compound interest.

The fourteenth rule is to learn to accept losses. No trader wins every time. Understand that losses are part of the game. If you give up after a loss, it's over. But if you learn from it and move forward, you become a true player.

The fifteenth rule is to develop the habit of winning. Make small wins a regular occurrence. Turn winning into a routine. When you feel like you're winning a little every day, your mind will start thinking accordingly. This mindset will take you to great heights.

Stepping into the trading field means accepting that the path isn't easy. It's tough, but not impossible. This path is for those who have the courage to change themselves and the passion to make these rules a part of their lives. When we touched upon the first fifteen rules, we saw that trading isn't just about charts and numbers—it's about the power of the mind, heart, and discipline. Now, let's dive deeper into these rules.

The first depth is that learning isn't a one-time task—it's a daily commitment. Think of going to the gym and working hard for one day, then resting for a year. Your body won't transform. Trading is the same. If you learn daily and take notes daily, your mind will grow stronger. The market plays new tricks every day, and you must learn new techniques daily. Only those who keep learning win.

The second depth lies in controlling your mind. Imagine the screen suddenly turns green, and everyone rushes to buy. Your heart will race. But the successful trader is the one who controls their racing heart. They know the crowd is often wrong. They know that letting emotions influence decisions will lead to losses. So, they sit, breathe, and act with a calm mind.

The third depth is risk management. Suppose you have $100,000. If you bet $50,000 on every trade, three mistakes will wipe you out. But if you risk only $2,000 per trade—just 2%—you can make 100 mistakes and still stay in the game. The player who lasts the longest wins, and risk management is what keeps the game going.

The fourth depth is discipline. Discipline isn't just about waking up on time or sitting at your desk. It's about following your strategy no matter what. Even if people mock you, even if impatience stirs within you, if you stick to your plan, the market will slowly turn your hard work into gold.

The fifth depth is learning to read the market's language. If you want to understand a language, you first learn its letters, then words, then sentences. Charts and patterns are the same. First, understand the meaning of a candlestick, then see how patterns connect, then grasp the story told by moving averages and volume. Slowly, the market will invite you into its depths, and one day, you'll be able to predict moves just by looking at a chart.

The sixth depth is keeping emotions at bay. Remember, trading isn't an emotional movie—it's a business. To win here, you need your brain, not your heart. Bets made in anger always lead to losses. Purchases made out of greed always cost more. Sales made out of fear always result in regret. So, train yourself to think like a machine. Keep a cool head and clear thoughts.

The seventh depth is adopting a long-term perspective. If you get caught up in daily fluctuations, you'll miss the bigger picture. The real player is the one who looks at weeks, months, and years. They understand that today's small loss is a stepping stone to tomorrow's big profit. They stay patient and committed to the path.

The eighth depth is making trading a lifestyle. If you only focus on trading while at your screen and forget about it once you step away, you're incomplete. The true trader brings discipline to every aspect of their life—sleep, focus, exercise. Their entire life becomes part of their trading strength.

The ninth depth is learning through practice. If you only read books and never step into the field, you'll never see the real game. Just as swimming can't be learned from a book, trading can't be learned without real money on the line. Start small, make mistakes, learn from them, and move forward. This is the real education.

The tenth depth is standing apart from the crowd. The crowd always makes noise, always rushes. But the true player watches calmly. They see where the crowd will get stuck and find their opportunity there. When everyone is buying, they observe. When everyone is selling, they look for chances. This ability to stand apart makes them a winner.

The eleventh depth is growing from small to big. Remember, every great trader started small. No one jumps straight to millions. Everyone began with small steps, small profits, small dreams. These small steps eventually lead to big victories. Never underestimate small beginnings—they pave the way to greatness.

The twelfth depth is sticking to your plan. Making a plan is easy, but sticking to it is hard. The market will shake you, scare you, tempt you. But you must do only what your plan says. If your entry point is decided, stick to it. If your stop-loss is set, follow it. If your target is fixed, hold onto it. This unwavering discipline is the true path to success.

The thirteenth depth is investing in yourself. Understand that knowledge is the greatest weapon. Spend money on books, courses, tools, and mentors. Learn something new every day. This investment in yourself will yield the highest returns.

The fourteenth depth is accepting losses. No one wins every time. Losses are part of the game. If you run from them, you'll break. If you learn from them, you'll grow stronger. This is the difference between ordinary people and winners.

The fifteenth depth is making winning a habit. People think winning is an accident. But in trading, winning is the result of hard work, learning, patience, and consistent decisions. If you make small, correct decisions every day, you'll achieve small wins daily. These small wins will build the habit of winning, and this habit will change your life.

Trading isn't just about money—it's a battle of the mind and discipline. If you're stepping into this battlefield, prepare your weapons: patience, discipline, learning, and confidence. Sharpen these weapons every day. Learning is the first and most important weapon. If you think you've learned everything, that's the biggest illusion. The market always asks new questions, and every question needs a new answer. Open charts daily, take notes daily, ask questions daily, and find answers daily. This continuous learning transforms you from ordinary to extraordinary.

Control your mind tightly. Remember, the market will tempt you with greed, crush you with fear, and provoke you with impatience. But the true player is the one who controls themselves every time. Just as a rider holds the reins of a horse tightly, you must hold the reins of your mind. If your mind pulls you, pull it back. If your mind rushes, stop it. This is true control.

Risk management isn't just a rule for money—it's a rule for peace of mind. If you bet big money all at once, you'll live in fear every second. But if you risk only a small portion, you'll watch calmly. This calmness will help you make the right decisions, and those decisions will lead to victory.

Discipline means having an iron will. Just as a soldier never breaks their training rules, a trader must never break their own rules. Whether the market rises or falls, whether friends pressure you or news influences you, you must always do what your discipline dictates. This unwavering commitment will set you apart.

Learn to read the market's language deeply. Charts aren't just numbers—they're mirrors of human emotions. A candlestick's shape shows whether people are greedy or fearful. A volume line reveals where the crowd is rushing. By reading this, you can see the future. The one who sees the future is the true player.

Keeping emotions at bay isn't easy, but it's essential. When your mind is free from emotions, every step you take is based on strategy. Anger, fear, greed, hope—keep them out. Keep only rules inside. This is true control. This is true victory.

Adopting a long-term perspective means staying committed to the path, no matter how many shocks come your way. Small losses, small fluctuations—they're all just tests. Success is also a test of patience. If you focus on small ups and downs, you'll never win the big game. But if you think long-term, the future will be yours.

Changing your lifestyle is the real secret. Winning in the market doesn't come from screen-time alone. Every habit outside the screen affects your decisions. Your sleep, your diet, your exercise, your routine—everything. If your lifestyle is disciplined, the market will be at your feet.

Practical steps are what make a trader a true master. Books show the way, mentors guide you. But the real game happens when you step into the field. When you put real money on the line, make mistakes, and learn from them. When you fall and rise again. This is the real learning.

Standing apart from the crowd takes courage. When everyone is rushing, selling, buying, you must stay calm. That's when real opportunities arise. If you sell out of fear or buy out of greed like the crowd, you'll get stuck. But if you think differently, you're on the path to becoming a true trader.

Starting small is the smart way because small trades give you experience. That experience slowly turns into millions. But if you bet big right away, you won't even get the chance to learn from your mistakes. The first mistake could be your last. Small steps are reliable ladders.

Following your plan is the hardest thing, but it's the most valuable. When the market scares you or tempts you, you must never step outside your plan. If your entry is decided, stick to it. If your stop-loss is set, follow it. If your target is fixed, hold onto it. This ironclad rule will turn into gold.

Investing in yourself means treating yourself as a gold mine. The money you spend on books, courses, tools, learning, and your mind is the money that will generate millions later. Stocks change, positions change, trends change. But if your understanding grows, you'll never lose.

Embracing losses is true strength. Those who reject losses miss out on lessons. Those who accept losses learn from them, and that learning turns into future victories. Without losses, victories are incomplete. Losses remind you that you're human. Victories show you that hard work can make you godlike.

Make winning a daily habit. Big wins come only after daily training with small wins. Small wins will give you confidence that you can do it. That confidence will make you bigger, and that big dream will take you to a place where earning millions feels normal.

The trading field can only be won by those who have transformed themselves. Before money, they change their mindset. Before hope, they develop patience. Before dreams, they change their thinking. This is the real game. This is the real goal.

Learning is an endless journey. Just as a river's water never stops flowing, a trader's learning should never stop. Every day, a new chart gives you a new lesson. Every day, a new pattern, a new clue, a new opportunity arises. If you keep learning, your books, notes, and mind will become a treasure of knowledge.

Control over your mind is the ultimate rule for victory. The market's movements will stir your emotions. But if you harness those emotions, they'll become the ladder to profit. Decide who the master of your mind is. If emotions take control, you'll lose. If you take control, you'll win in every situation.

Risk management will save you every time. No one can be 100% correct in the market. But risk management gives you the power to stay in the game 100% of the time. Playing with small risks and aiming big is the smart way. Controlling risk every time is true discipline. This is your shield.

Discipline will keep you standing firm when everyone else wavers. The market will shake you, social media will scare you, friends will give advice, TV news will scream. But if you stay disciplined, you'll stand strong amidst all the mistakes. This iron discipline will set you apart.

Learn to read the market's language deeply. Charts aren't just numbers—they're mirrors of human emotions. A candlestick's shape shows whether people are greedy or fearful. A volume line reveals where the crowd is rushing. By reading this, you can see the future. The one who sees the future is the true player.

Keeping emotions at bay isn't easy, but it's essential. When your mind is free from emotions, every step you take is based on strategy. Anger, fear, greed, hope—keep them out. Keep only rules inside. This is true control. This is true victory.

Adopting a long-term perspective means staying committed to the path, no matter how many shocks come your way. Small losses, small fluctuations—they're all just tests. Success is also a test of patience. If you focus on small ups and downs, you'll never win the big game. But if you think long-term, the future will be yours.

Changing your lifestyle is the real secret. Winning in the market doesn't come from screen-time alone. Every habit outside the screen affects your decisions. Your sleep, your diet, your exercise, your routine—everything. If your lifestyle is disciplined, the market will be at your feet.

Practical steps are what make a trader a true master. Books show the way, mentors guide you. But the real game happens when you step into the field. When you put real money on the line, make mistakes, and learn from them. When you fall and rise again. This is the real learning.

Standing apart from the crowd takes courage. When everyone is rushing, selling, buying, you must stay calm. That's when real opportunities arise. If you sell out of fear or buy out of greed like the crowd, you'll get stuck. But if you think differently, you're on the path to becoming a true trader.

Starting small is the smart way because small trades give you experience. That experience slowly turns into millions. But if you bet big right away, you won't even get the chance to learn from your mistakes. The first mistake could be your last. Small steps are reliable ladders.

Following your plan is the hardest thing, but it's the most valuable. When the market scares you or tempts you, you must never step outside your plan. If your entry is decided, stick to it. If your stop-loss is set, follow it. If your target is fixed, hold onto it. This ironclad rule will turn into gold.

Investing in yourself means treating yourself as a gold mine. The money you spend on books, courses, tools, learning, and your mind is the money that will generate millions later. Stocks change, positions change, trends change. But if your understanding grows, you'll never lose.

Embracing losses is true strength. Those who reject losses miss out on lessons. Those who accept losses learn from them, and that learning turns into future victories. Without losses, victories are incomplete. Losses remind you that you're human. Victories show you that hard work can make you godlike.

Make winning a daily habit. Big wins come only after daily training with small wins. Small wins will give you confidence that you can do it. That confidence will make you bigger, and that big dream will take you to a place where earning millions feels normal.

The trading field can only be won by those who have transformed themselves. Before money, they change their mindset. Before hope, they develop patience. Before dreams, they change their thinking. This is the real game. This is the real goal.

Thank you